The Selective Mutism Treatment Guide

Manuals for Parents, Teachers, and Therapists

still waters run deep

Ruth Perednik

Oaklands

**We would like to hear from you.
Please contact us at:
SMTreatmentCenter@gmail.com**

ISBN: 9659178301
ISBN-13: 978-9659178308

First edition published 2011
Library of Congress Cataloging-in-Publication data.
Perednik Ruth
The Selective Mutism Treatment Guide:
For Parents, Teachers, and Therapists *Still Waters Run Deep*

Oaklands

Jerusalem

**For Mum
my compass, always**

Contents

Introduction:

How to Use These Manuals

Before you is an innovative, tried and tested approach to the treatment of selective mutism (SM)—the consistent failure to speak in certain settings or to specific people despite having the ability to understand and use language. It is based on twenty years of clinical experience with hundreds of children with SM, and on current, widely accepted ways of understanding and treating this condition. It views parents, school staff, and therapists as having the potential to successfully implement this treatment and free their child of selective mutism. Children with SM usually respond well to the appropriate treatment and break free of their silent shackles in a relatively short-term intervention program. What's more, most of them become regular, normative children once they overcome selective mutism.

In this treatment guide, **parents, school staff, and therapists each have a treatment manual written specifically for them.** Each manual includes an overview of how to understand and treat SM, as well as insights, strategies, and tools specific to each one. Parents and teachers are vital, active partners, and are each guided to engage in activities aimed at helping the child to speak freely. For therapists, a clear, step-by-step guide to the program will assist them to implement an effective treatment plan.

This treatment plan may be carried out by a therapist, a family member, a teacher, or any other person who is sufficiently warm, skilled, understanding, and committed to the well-being of the child with SM. Many concerned and caring parents have implemented this program without a therapist, and teachers too will find much that they can do to help the child in school without the full-scale program. However, when the resources and the inclination are there to implement the complete program with parents, teachers, and therapist working together—cooperating, communicating, and fine-tuning one another's interventions—the result is a potent push toward overcoming SM.

This approach is based on two main underlying components. Firstly, it is designed to enable the child to move as seamlessly as possible between the various frameworks in which he lives—home, school and the outside world—in a harmonious way. This is reflected in the locations at which the therapy takes place—at home and in school. The child's home functioning is harnessed and then generalized to the school or kindergarten.

The therapist's intervention begins with structured sessions in the child's home with family members and the therapist, in a light, playful, and natural atmosphere, during which the child is gradually eased into speech with the therapist. Usually the child with SM is less hampered by his anxiety at home than in school or kindergarten, and so can express who he really is. This optimum functioning of the child with SM at his home is frequently at a level of verbal communication and social interaction that is literally unbelievable to those who see him only in school. Once the child is speaking to the therapist at home, the location of the sessions is moved to the kindergarten or school, initially with the therapist and later on including friends and staff, with the aim of enabling the child to speak to everyone in school. In this way, the treatment acts as a bridge to facilitate transferring and generalizing his selectively optimum level of functioning from his home to all his daily environments.

This leads us to the second underlying component: deep respect and belief in the child's nature and his home environment. The aim is not to change him, but rather to build on his and his family's strengths. Thus the school may look at ways to emulate the factors that enable the child to function well at home, while the parents will be incorporating insights and modes of functioning aimed at lowering the child's anxiety levels and helping him acquire long-term coping skills that will enable the child to function well outside the home.

This treatment method is designed to increase the speed and effectiveness of therapy. The initial home-based therapy and ongoing involvement of the parents aims to render redundant long periods of therapy that are called for when treatment takes place in a therapist's office or only in the school. Its aim is not just to have a pleasant, even enlightening hour per week in a therapist's office, but rather to improve the child's functioning and well-being on a daily, hourly basis—in school, at home, and in the world at large! It is designed to be a satisfying and empowering experience for the child and his family.

The three manuals have been created to be used independently. This means that there is some overlap. For example, the definition and causes of selective mutism are repeated, albeit with some differences, in all three manuals. It is recommended that the parents and the therapist read all three manuals, in order to be aware of the variety of potential tools and strategies that may be used, and so that they can oversee and coordinate the interventions of all those involved.

For the sake of clarity, the therapist and teacher are referred to as feminine, while children with selective mutism are referred to as masculine; in practice, SM affects both girls and boys. The guide is geared toward the younger child, up until the pre-teen stage. Appendix 2 (page 118) includes guidelines for adapting this approach to meet the needs of the older child.

The manuals are designed so that a complete treatment schedule, including sessions with a therapist along with parental and teacher interventions, can be carried out. Frequently this broad (and effective) treatment is either thought not to be necessary, or the human resources required are not available. When this is the case, parents and teachers can help the child by utilizing strategies outlined in the manuals within a narrower treatment plan.

For example, a teacher may carry out a treatment plan based on a combination of what is written in the therapist's and teacher's manuals. The teacher might begin with several home visits during which she eases the child into speech with her, according to the home-sessions steps outlined in the Therapist's Manual. After this she might hold regular short sessions with the child in the school where she eases the child from nonverbal communication, to pre-direct speech (for example, listening to recordings), and ultimately to direct speech as explained in the Teacher's Manual. Likewise, a parent may implement several treatment strategies described and explained in the Parents' Manual, such as holding regular talking-playing sessions in the kindergarten, initially working on building up the child's verbal output with the parent alone, and then gradually increasing the number of children and staff participating in these sessions.

Raising awareness of the causes and treatment of selective mutism is vital. As with most dysfunctions that are anxiety-based and result in "acting in"—introversion, avoidance, and timidity, as opposed to "acting out" when the child is literally screaming for help—SM is often left untreated as the child may cause little disruption to the kindergarten or school. This is not to say that there is no suffering— the child always suffers profoundly as a result of his SM, as do his concerned parents.

Failure to treat SM is all the more lamentable as SM is usually highly responsive to treatment. Early intervention can avoid a host of residual effects on the child's emotional well-being, and may re-channel the child's development onto a more regular, adaptive track. Usually a child freed from the shackles of his silence feels a surge of confidence, competence, and well-being, the emotional ripples reaching distant shores.

The Selective Mutism Treatment Guide

Parents' Manual

still waters run deep

Contents of Parents' Manual

Introduction to Parents' Manual

In all probability, you are reading this manual because your child or someone you care for fails to talk in select settings. This manual is a part of a comprehensive treatment program, which includes a manual for parents, teachers, and therapists. Ideally, your child will be assisted to gradually learn to speak normally in all situations by these three sectors. For each one of these people, their task is separate and interconnected, with the joint goal of helping your child to communicate socially in a regular way. It is highly recommended that you read all three of the manuals, so you will be fully aware of all that can be done to help your child and you will be able to provide input on how to fine-tune this program to your child's needs.

You, as the parent, know your child the best! The teacher and therapist need your guidance as to your understanding of your child, his thoughts and feelings, and his functioning at home and in the world at large. Your collaboration is vital through all stages of the treatment, from assessment, understanding the child's background, the treatment stages, to maintaining the child's progress in the future. As a parent, your concern for your child's welfare is paramount; to this end you have the role of working as a team with the therapist and teacher in the framework of this three-way intervention, with distinct tasks that will be outlined in this manual. It is most conducive to success when a respectful, open, and communicative relationship exists between parents, teacher, and therapist so that each corner of this triumvirate can contribute his expertise while simultaneously gaining and adjusting his understanding by the insights of his colleagues in this enterprise.

This treatment program is based on several principles, which will become clear on an operative level as you read the manual. It aims to build bridges between the diverse settings in which your child lives, enabling him to move seamlessly between contexts. In other words, it aims to understand what allows him to speak at home and to try to incorporate those elements at school so that he will feel more comfortable there. At the same time, some factors at school may be conducive to assertiveness and independence, and the parents may wish to incorporate these factors at some level at home. This outlook is reflected in the locations of the therapy—at home and at school.

In addition, the treatment plan incorporates what is widely accepted today about treating selective mutism: that behavioral methods with cognitive components are thought to be most effective for SM, that it is frequently anxiety-based, and that the family and school should be intimately involved in any course of treatment. This program has been developed out of the clinical experience of treating hundreds of children with SM.

Sometimes it is not feasible, or it is thought not to be necessary, to utilize the complete treatment program—for example, if no therapist can be found to work with the child in school or if it is felt that that the teacher could carry out the stages of therapy herself. In such cases, the program can be adapted to incorporate such human recourses as are available; parents and teachers may work together to build a plan including the steps outlined in the three manuals.

These treatment manuals are designed in a way so that when time is tight, each may be read and its treatment plan implemented without the necessity of reading the other two manuals. For this reason, there is some overlap—the definition and causes of SM are repeated in each manual, albeit with some modifications. Whenever time allows, reading all three manuals is advised—it will give you a full picture of the suggested treatment strategies.

What is Selective Mutism?

Selective mutism (SM) is a childhood social communication disorder in which children consistently fail to speak in select situations despite their ability to understand and use language. Children with SM usually speak to family members at home but do not speak at kindergarten or school. The speech patterns of each child with SM vary along a continuum of severity—from children who speak to everyone outside school and to select peers in school, to children who are unable to speak to everyone in school, including peers and staff. Some will not speak to anyone outside their home or only to certain family members inside their home, and a rare few do not speak to family members inside the home. Often there is a marked contrast between the outgoing and communicative child at home and the inhibited, introverted functioning at school.

When another condition exists that accounts better for the failure to speak, such as pervasive developmental disorder, retardation, psychosis, or a lack of language skills, then the child is not considered to have SM.

There are additional traits that research has found to be associated with SM; again, each child has a unique set of characteristics. Research studies have found that around 90% of children with SM suffer from social anxiety, and 30–40% have some language or speech impairment. Other associated conditions could include shyness and hypersensitivity, oppositional behavior, stubbornness and perfectionism, neuro-developmental disorder or delay (often auditory processing delay), and learning disabilities.

There is often a genetic component of shyness or a history of SM in one of the child's parents or siblings. In addition, bilingualism and disconnectedness from the cultural milieu of the outside society are sometimes found in the families of children with SM.

No link has been found between intelligence and SM, and no link has been found in the large research studies between traumatic events and SM. For a sensitive, anxious child, seemingly everyday events may be experienced as traumatic, such as being shouted at by a teacher, being embarrassed in front of a class, or being mocked by peers for a mispronunciation.

Most research has found that the incidence of SM is around 0.7% or seven children in every one thousand, and it has been found to be three times that number in children from bilingual homes. It is most prevalent between the ages of four and eight; onset usually occurs when the child first enters an educational framework in which speech is expected, but sometimes onset is gradual—the child's speech output diminishes until he eventually stops speaking.

What Causes Selective Mutism?

Selective mutism is caused by the interaction between the nature of the child and external factors—nature and nurture. One can conceptualize this as various factors fitting into one of three groups: predisposing factors, triggers, and maintaining factors.

Predisposing factors include elements of the child's psychological and physiological makeup that cause him to be more vulnerable to selective mutism. This could include an anxious or shy nature, stubbornness and perfectionism, or a family history of shyness. Many children with SM have some type of speech difficulty, including having less confidence in their expressive language due to their bilingualism.

When there is a combination of predisposing factors that heighten the child's vulnerability to SM, along with triggers—events such as kindergarten admission or a geographical move—the scales can tip and bring about the onset of SM.

Predisposing factors:

- Child's anxiety, shyness, timidity, hyper-sensitivity
- Family history of shyness, anxiety, or selective mutism—can include anxious parents, anxious behavior modeling by parents
- Speech impairment of child—usually expressive language
- Bilingualism and disconnectedness from the predominant culture
- Neuro-developmental disorder or delay, often auditory processing disorder

Triggers:

- School or kindergarten admission
- Frequent geographical moves
- Family moving to area with different spoken language
- Negative reactions to child talking—bullying, shouting, mocking etc.

Maintaining factors:

- Social isolation of families
- Misdiagnosis (oppositional behavior, autism, retardation)
- Lack of early and appropriate intervention
- Lack of understanding by teachers, families, psychologists
- Reinforcement by increased attention or affection
- Heightened anxiety levels caused by pressure to speak
- Ability to convey messages nonverbally
- Lack of belief in ability to overcome SM

Maintaining factors facilitate the continuation of the condition—potentially slowing the child's recovery from selective mutism. For example, if SM is misdiagnosed in school as oppositional behavior, and is therefore not given appropriate treatment, or if there is great pressure on the child to speak which heightens his anxiety levels and paradoxically makes it harder for him to speak, then the duration of the SM may be lengthened. (Adapted from Shipon-Blum 2007.)

How Selective Mutism Can Affect Your Child and Your Family

While each child and all families are unique and respond to SM in their own way, certain feelings and reactions are common. One thing is almost always the case with a child who is not speaking (usually) in kindergarten or school: a child with SM suffers! He cannot be himself—the more spontaneous, communicative child he is in other contexts. He must expend effort to ensure that his radar informing him of who is in his proximity is always on, and control himself so that when his private space is encroached or when he is in a setting in which he does not speak, he stays quiet. High and constant energy expenditure is required to maintain this awareness and control. This in itself is distressing, however effortless the child with SM appears to make it.

The lack of verbal communication causes the child to miss out on social and learning experiences which would further his development. A child who cannot say what he wants will frequently be included in activities he wishes to avoid and conversely will be excluded from experiences he desperately wants to have. This is a recipe for frustration. This frustration is often taken out on his family when he returns home and can finally express himself. Sometimes the frustration expresses itself in school, as the child makes his presence felt with his hands, not his voice.

When a child with SM is unfortunate enough to be in a context in which he is misunderstood and considered to be unintelligent, unable to communicate, or oppositional, he may be inappropriately labeled and consequently placed in an unsuitable learning environment. This generally exacerbates the child's difficulties.

Parents confronted with a child who fails to speak in school frequently go through a period of heightened anxiety themselves. The parents' concern for their child and their grappling with schools and possible interventions, as well as their long-term projections and postulations regarding future implications for their beloved child, can be overwhelming. To make matters worse, the parents' posturing to get appropriate intervention for their child can be misconstrued as over protectiveness and identified by the school as the cause, not the effect, of the child's SM.

For all these reasons (and many more), early intervention is vital. What's more, it usually works! Response to intervention using behavioral therapies for children with SM has been found to be highly effective. In addition, the following treatment plan is generally experienced by the child as an enjoyable, satisfying experience; once children break the barriers and speak, they usually experience a surge of self-confidence.

How to Talk to Your Child about Selective Mutism

Selective mutism is usually anxiety-based and that must be borne in mind when talking to your child. **One of the aims of discussing speech difficulties with your child is to lower his anxiety levels.** However you choose to express it semantically, the message should be: "We love you exactly as you are. Right now you can't speak in some situations or to some people, but we know that soon you will overcome it and be able to speak." In other words, you are telling your child three things:

1. **You are not anxious about his SM.**
2. **You accept him as he is.**
3. **You have total confidence that he will overcome his SM soon.**

Other family members (siblings, grandparents, etc.) should adopt a similar stance. This bolsters the child's confidence that he has the strength and courage to speak, and your apparent lack of worry will do wonders for lowering his anxiety level. Paradoxically, the more he feels your concern and is pressured to speak, the harder it will be for him to talk, as his anxiety level will rise. Lowering his anxiety level regarding speech is usually prerequisite for enabling speech.

Constant checking as to whether he spoke in kindergarten or school and to whom, transmits to him your anxiety and makes him more anxious. Similarly, prizes offered for speech, or punishments for non-speech are contraindicated—they too may increase your child's anxiety level.

You do not need to try to increase your child's motivation to speak. As explained in the previous section, SM causes suffering and frustration in children, and every child with SM that I have encountered desperately wants to speak.

Another productive message to convey to your child is the normalization of SM. He can be told that many children find it hard to speak in school, are wonderful children, and overcome their SM in time. This is often a relief for a child who may see himself as different or problematic. During therapy, the child can be told that many children have been helped by sessions such as those he is having in school. This should not be said at the beginning of therapy, but rather after it has gotten underway and it is clear to the child that its aim is social communication.

After these two messages have been conveyed to your child, do not engage him in ongoing discussion about SM unless he initiates it. Your frequent discussion of SM may cause him to feel more pressure to speak and in fact make it harder for him to progress.

How to Treat Selective Mutism

It is widely accepted today that the aim of treatment for SM should be to help the child to speak in all his daily environments to all people. Behavioral treatment with cognitive components is generally considered to be the most effective way to remove the symptom of selective mutism. SM is usually anxiety-based and any treatment plan must take this into consideration. It is most conducive to rapid recovery when the family and school are intimately involved in any course of treatment. In order for this to happen, it is vital to establish an open, communicative, and mutually respectful relationship between the teacher, the parents, and the therapist.

This guide is presented as a comprehensive treatment plan for therapist, parents, and teachers—each with their own tasks but working in conjunction with one another. This is in an ideal situation where there are the resources and the will to tackle SM from all three directions. However, if a full-scale intervention is not possible, or it is thought that it is not called for, then this treatment plan offers a variety of ideas, interventions, and activities that can be implemented by the teacher, parent, or therapist alone, without the full-scale program. In many cases, a partial implementation of the program can bring desirable results and is often sufficient to help the child to overcome selective mutism.

Overview of Therapy

The therapy outlined before you is a behavioral plan that aims to **remove the symptom of failure to speak** in certain settings. I believe that especially with young children, symptom removal is paramount, because the symptom can affect the child's social, language, and learning development, as well as exerting a powerful influence on how the child feels about himself—his self-confidence, his social self-image, and his view of himself as "normal." In addition to this aim of facilitating speech, during the assessment stage other issues may be found that can be addressed within this therapy—for example, independence, assertiveness, and anxiety within the family. These may be incorporated as aims within the therapy, as part of the parents', teacher's, and therapist's interventions.

In some cases, children with SM have additional issues other than difficulty speaking in select places or to certain people. Some have speech impediments, and others may have additional anxiety conditions, which may require specific treatment beyond the scope of this plan. Once the failure to speak is remedied, the child will be more able to participate in the requisite treatment for other difficulties should they exist.

When a child successfully overcomes SM, this in itself has a powerful self-affirming effect. The child learns that he has the courage to overcome difficulties, and this can have a ripple effect on further problems the child may have, especially anxiety-related issues.

Prior to the start of treatment, the therapist should meet with the parents and teacher in order to assess the child's speech patterns, his strengths and difficulties, and other factors relating to SM. After the assessment is completed, therapy sessions with the child will begin while guidance will be given simultaneously to the teacher and the parents. The therapist will explain the therapy outline to the parents and will give ongoing updates regarding progress once therapy has started. Three-way meetings involving the therapist, school staff, and parents should be held at regular intervals.

Here follows a summary of the therapist's sessions with the child, then the teacher's interventions will be outlined, and then I will focus on what you as a parent can do to help your child overcome selective mutism.

The Stages of Therapy: Home-Based, School-Based

A primary aim of the therapy is to build on the child's optimum functioning, which is usually at the home, facilitating similar behavior in other surroundings. As such, the **therapy begins, whenever possible, at home.** The aim of these home sessions is to reach the stage wherein the child speaks directly and comfortably to the therapist.

In the initial (usually between two and six) sessions in the child's home, the therapist engages in minimal small talk with the parent, trying to be unobtrusive to the child. The initial aim is that the child speaks in the presence of the therapist. Gradually over the course of the home sessions, the therapist plays with the child and other family members and finally directs speech to the child and plays with him alone. By the end of the home sessions stage of the program, the child should be speaking directly with the therapist.

In the final home session, the therapist explains to the child that she works with children in schools, and that she intends to have sessions with the child in school in the coming weeks. In these sessions she will play with the child, sometimes together with other children, and hopefully help him to feel comfortable and enjoy school. (With older children a more cognitive-behavioral method is used, including open discussion about the difficulty speaking as outlined in Appendix 2 of the Therapist's Manual on page 118. With children up to around third grade, a more behavioral approach is usually recommended.)

Once the child speaks to the therapist in the home, the **therapy is moved to the school**. Therapy then takes place one to three times a week in a designated room in the school. Initially, the aim of the sessions is that the child speaks to the therapist in the therapy room in school; activities include games conducive to speech, listening to recordings of the child from home, and arts and crafts. The activities included in these sessions are adapted in accordance with the child's preferences.

Usually this transfer of location goes smoothly, and the child continues to speak to the therapist in the school therapy room. Occasionally, the child is reticent to speak in the new school setting. If this is the case, the therapist employs a variety of tools to facilitate speech. This could include recording the child at home and playing the recording in the school sessions, and including a sibling or inviting the parents to participate in the initial school sessions. There are also behavioral tools that can be used, such as the "sliding in" technique, a form of stimulus shaping developed by Johnson and Wintgens (2001). Here the parent is alone with the child in the schoolroom, and the child speaks to him or her. Then a game is played involving rote speech and some physical activity—for example, the parent and child throw a ball between them and each time the thrower says a number. In small but sure stages, the therapist gradually comes within hearing range of the game, eventually enters the room, and finally participates in the game. All these techniques and strategies are explained fully in the Therapist's Manual.

Once the child is speaking comfortably to the therapist in school, **the generalization stage** takes place. Here the aim is **to broaden the child's speaking habits** to include as many people as possible—initially within the therapy room at school. The therapist invites classmates and staff to join in the sessions in small steps, employing behavioral techniques when necessary.

Once the child is speaking to several people in the therapy room, the next stage is to broaden the range of settings in which the child speaks. In order to achieve this the sessions are moved either to an open space in the school, such as a hall or play area, or to a corner in the classroom itself. Here, using the same methods of playing, recording, and other activities used up to now, the child is enabled to speak in the classroom setting. Usually, as the child progresses in therapy, spontaneous progress is seen simultaneously in other settings. For example, when the child starts speaking in the sessions to a number of children, it is likely that he will speak to some of these children in recess, or perhaps quietly in the classroom.

Teacher's Interventions

The beauty of this program is its comprehensiveness. It is designed to assist the child in the main settings of his life with a three-pronged intervention: parents, teachers, and therapist who simultaneously strive to assist the child to overcome his difficulty. When all three sectors act in coordination, the effect is powerful. While the therapy is ongoing, both the parents and the teacher will be carrying out their own interventions aimed at helping the child to speak.

The teacher may assess the child's functioning at school, and consider how to help him in five areas:

1. Encouraging a communicative relationship between the teacher and child, initially nonverbal, ultimately verbal
2. Lowering the child's anxiety level in school
3. Helping him interact socially with other children
4. Building his independence, assertiveness, and self-esteem in school, and not exempting him from activities because of the SM
5. Blurring the differentiation the child has made between home and school functioning

The teachers' interventions are fully described in the Teacher's Manual. Here I will give a few examples to illustrate the above points.

Sometimes, when a child fails to speak, the educational staff feel that they do not have the ability to develop a communicative relationship with the child. In this program teachers are encouraged and guided so that they build a warm, supportive, communicative, nonverbal relationship, which is a precursor of verbal contact between child and teacher. The teacher may be guided in developing a structured behavior modification plan for her to implement within the framework of the warm reciprocal relationship she will have developed with the child. This requires a few minutes daily on the part of the teacher, and is usually most effective when accompanied by guidance and coaching following each teacher-child session (even by phone, a few minutes a day) by the therapist.

This social contact with the teacher plays a fundamental role in easing the anxiety level of the child, as now the child can express to the teacher issues that may be upsetting him, such as bullying, social pressures, and academic concerns. He may request changes that could make him more comfortable at school, such as sitting next to a friend. Another vital key to lowering the child's anxiety level in school is that the staff does not put pressure on the child to speak.

The teacher can encourage social interaction with peers by placing the child in small groups of children who seem a good match for him and whom he likes. He might be given a special position or lead a project in an area he likes and is good at.

Finally, contact between the home and school is vital, including home visits, utilizing the parents' understanding of the child, and thinking together with the parents and therapist about elements that could make the child feel more at home in school.

The importance of the teacher's fluid contact with the parents and therapist is a cornerstone of success; each of the three active parties in the treatment must mutually fine-tune the other parties' interventions, communicating progress and setbacks as well as appraisals of what more can be done. This can take place in prearranged meetings at set intervals and be supplemented by weekly phone conversations. When the significant adults in all of the main contexts in the child's life are working together toward a common aim, the effect is powerful; the whole is far more potent than the sum total of its parts.

Parents' Interventions and Tasks

I have seen many concerned and able parents carry out structured treatment plans that have cured or significantly eased their child's selective mutism. Here follow interventions specific to the parents, which may be carried out in conjunction with the therapist and/or teacher.

1. Assessment

The first three points are relevant when a therapist is implementing a treatment plan. Prior to the start of treatment, a comprehensive assessment is made, in which the therapist collates information from the home and school in order to estimate the level of functioning and the emotional state of the child, as well as his strengths and abilities and any additional difficulties. This process is important in order to tailor the therapy to your child. The parents, as the greatest experts on their child, are indispensable contributors to the evaluation.

2. Home therapy sessions

Once the initial therapy sessions begin in the home, the parents facilitate and conduct them together with the therapist. They plan who is to be present, they set the time and place of the sessions, and they ensure that the activities in these sessions are enjoyable and appropriate. Parents must provide recording devices, which are to be used in the home sessions and in between meetings, as well as in the school-based therapy sessions. In short, parents work together with the therapist to ensure the success of the home sessions.

3. School therapy sessions

Similarly, when the therapy sessions take place in the school, the parents' cooperation is required. Frequently parents are requested to help in preparing homework for sessions, which is usually taping recordings or films of the child at home. Sometimes an impasse occurs at a transitional stage in the school-based therapy, and a family member is requested to come to one or more school sessions to facilitate speech in school. In such a case, the parent's help is required to plan and conduct the sessions with the therapist.

4. School-based talking-playing sessions

Whenever possible, whether or not treatment with a therapist is being implemented, it is recommended that parents go to the child's school or nursery between one and three times a week for short, enjoyable talking-playing sessions. These are informal sessions in which the parent plays and talks with her child in school or nursery. This can be done in the morning when the parent drops the child off at school before the school day begins, or at any other time that is convenient for parent and teacher. The parent considers where in the school the child will speak to her, which depends on the severity of the SM. Some children will speak with a parent or family member in a secluded corner of the class, while others need the security of a closed room in order to speak to the parent.

These sessions significantly boost the effectiveness of the therapy. For example, instead of the child speaking once a week in school during one hour in therapy with the therapist, he is now speaking up to four times a week in school—three times with a family member and once with the therapist. The therapist may guide the parent (after consultation with the teacher) regarding the location of the sessions and the possible inclusion of other children in the sessions.

Here is a concrete example to illustrate such a session: A mother (or father or sibling) might come twice a week to the child's kindergarten, sit in a secluded corner with the child, and play with Play-Doh for twenty minutes as other children come into the nursery. If the child speaks to his mother, he may continue doing so even after other children come within hearing range and eventually when they sit with him at the table. Another example could be of a child who will not speak to a parent in the regular classroom; he may have these sessions with his parent in a closed, private room in the school, perhaps inviting a friend with whom he talks outside school to join in. As he grows freer in his speech in these sessions with his parent and friend, additional friends may join in, and so his circle of peers with whom he speaks in school will be widened.

In order to maximize the effectiveness of these sessions, they should be planned with the therapist and the teacher so that they complement the concurrent stages of therapy and classroom functioning. They will be structured according to the same behavioral principles used in the therapist's interventions. Initially the child will speak to the parent in a private area, then the circle with whom he speaks will be gradually enlarged to include friends and/or staff, and finally his speech will be generalized to include additional settings in the school, such as public areas and the classroom. The aim is to enable him to speak to everyone in all settings. Parents who are implementing this program without a therapist's simultaneous intervention or guidance should read through the Therapist's Manual in order to understand how to build a structured behavioral plan with small steps that shape and generalize the child's speech.

5. Inviting friends home, telephone calls, recordings

Inviting classmates home to play can considerably help your child to overcome SM. If he speaks to his friend at your home, then a big barrier will have been broken—the classmate will have heard his voice—and that will make it easier for him to speak freely in school. And if more friends come, and he speaks to them too, this will further advance his progress. Even if he fails to speak to his friends at home, but communicates nonverbally and enjoys their company, this will facilitate greater social competence in school.

Friends should be chosen who suit your child's personality and whom he likes. The teacher can advise you as to whom she considers to be compatible. When these play-dates take place, do all you can to ensure that they are enjoyable and go smoothly. A socially shy child may need some behind-the-scenes assistance. You could plan an enjoyable activity, a special or new game, an outing, or some attractive arts and crafts activity. You can also help ensure that the house is peaceful and that any antagonistic siblings (if an issue) are otherwise engaged. If your child has nurturing, fun siblings, it may be preferable for them to be present! Frequent, enjoyable play-dates truly facilitate beating SM.

Telephone calls may be a first step in verbal communication with schoolmates and staff; encourage your child to speak on the phone to people with whom he already speaks freely face-to-face, and suggest calling staff or classmates with whom he has not yet spoken, if and when you feel your child is ready.

At the onset of therapy, it is worthwhile to purchase a taping device and play with it at home. In all likelihood it will prove productive. Recordings are a useful pre-direct speech step where a child's voice is present without him having to speak directly. Playing around with recording devices at home—MP3, office tapes, talking photo albums, taping on cell phones and cameras—often proves invaluable to therapy. Once your child enjoys playing with the tape at home with family members, it can be incorporated into therapy. If he does not object, the tape could be played to friends when they come to play, perhaps making it easier for your child to speak naturally once his friends have heard his voice.

6. Desensitization outside school

The behavioral techniques used by the teacher, the parents and the therapist in school, may be required to help your child speak in settings or with people outside school. If your child does not manage to talk to friends at home, you may utilize a behavior modification program that you can implement at home which will take your child from silence to speech in small structured steps. After the initial assessment of your child and in your intermittent meetings with the therapist and teacher, it will be apparent with whom the child has difficulty speaking. The therapist can help you plan the desensitization schedule in order to begin speaking to such a person. This is a scale of steps to gradually approach speech; for example, first nonverbal communication, then playing a tape of the child speaking, followed by speaking on the phone, and finally using a "sliding in" technique (as described earlier).

To give a theoretical example: The first step at home may be inviting a friend and playing a prerecorded tape of the child speaking with his family in the presence of the friend, followed by a game of catch played with the parent, child and his friend, requiring sound production, such as saying "shhhhh" or whistling each time you throw the ball. Once this is successfully played the small group may play Chinese whispers; initially the child whispers only to the family member, later also to the friend. Then a game of snap could be played in which when the child gets a card identical to that of another player, he says "snap". Some children will pass through all these stages in one play-date, others may require at least one session to master each task. When several sessions are required, the previously achieved games are played before attempting to master a new goal. The games should be played in a light and playful atmosphere, as this will help your child to keep his anxiety in check.

Many determined, dedicated parents have learned to implement these behavior modification programs at home successfully; thus, they have a series of steps they can implement at home that enables their child to gradually speak to friends. Often the child understands that this series of games offers him a bridge that takes him from silence to speech, and so he gladly embraces the procedure that offers him a way to speak to friends or relatives at home.

A further example of desensitization carried out by the parents outside school could be a child who doesn't speak to his grandparents or uncles and requires help in gradually speaking to them. A plan could be constructed in which the child first plays and shows his relative a talking album in which he has previously recorded himself describing the pictures in the album; followed by leaving reciprocal messages on a cell phone; after which the child speaks directly on the cell phone; and finally he speaks face to face.

Another example could be a desensitization schedule for a child who doesn't speak to waiters in a restaurant. The child could go with his parent once a week to a restaurant as a special treat; the first time, he points to "milkshake" on the menu to communicate his choice to the waiter; the next week he plays a prepared tape of himself saying "milkshake please"; and finally he says "milkshake." These are just examples, the structure and pace would be designed to fit the needs of each child, with a family member carrying out the desensitization procedure.

7. Lowering anxiety

An underlying premise of the treatment of SM is that the disorder is usually anxiety-based, so in order to free the child of SM, effort must be made in all settings to lower the child's anxiety levels.

At home, this translates into easing the pressure on the child to speak. Paradoxically, the more a child is coaxed to speak, the harder it may be for him to do so. This will express itself in how you speak to your child (see the earlier section "How to Talk to Your Child about Selective Mutism", page 12). Make clear to your child your manifest confidence that he will overcome SM. In all of the interventions described here, the lighter and more playful the tone, the more effective they will be in lowering the child's anxiety. As mentioned before, positive and negative pressure—both reprimanding a child and promising prizes for speech—may cause the child to be more anxious about his difficulty speaking.

8. Modeling

Parents must try to show their child that they are not overly anxious about the SM. It is natural that every parent of a child with SM is anxious about it, therefore parents may need to work on their own anxiety management, too. How parents cope with anxiety is a strong modeling example for their child.

Research has found that often (but not always) one of the parents of a child with SM has some anxiety issues herself. If you feel that you have anxiety that is affecting your parenting, this is an opportunity for you to discuss it with the therapist. You will not only improve your parenting skills, but also show your child how you are overcoming your fears, engendering a feeling of empowerment in the family. You might learn some cognitive-behavioral tips on how to work toward lowering your anxiety about SM. Two examples of cognitive-behavioral exercises are given in the worksheets at the end of this section (pages 30-31).

Similarly, modeling social behavior can be very powerful. For example, if your family is fairly insular, and you work on opening your home to visitors, this may encourage your child to be more open to receiving his friends at home.

9. Increasing independence — enabling as opposed to protecting

When a parent sees his child feeling scared or anxious, it is his natural instinct to try and protect him from the perceived danger. And when there is an immediate extreme danger, it is indeed the parent's duty to protect his child, to pull him away from exposed electricity, for example.

However, with anxiety-provoking everyday situations in which the child needs to learn to function in order to lead a full and satisfying life, the parents' aim should be to enable him to acquire and practice coping skills. This involves conveying to the child your belief in his abilities and allowing him to be in situations that are challenging to a tolerable degree and will give him the experience needed to hone his skills. For example, when a shy child is asked a question by an acquaintance, it is tempting for the parent to answer for the child. But if the child, with some effort and a little discomfort, can answer, then the parent is depriving him of a valuable social skills building experience by answering in his place. There is a fine line between not asking a child to do something that raises his anxiety to an unbearable level, and encouraging him to express himself in tolerably anxiety-producing situations. If this is a relevant issue for you and your child, then it may be helpful to work with the therapist to consider how to discern and apply the fine line between enabling and protecting. Useful further reading is listed in the reference section.

In addition, at the age at which SM is most prevalent—around the beginning of elementary school—children are becoming more independent, functioning in large educational institutions, some traveling on school buses. Parents can assist their children by fostering appropriate levels of independence at home. This can include tasks such as tidying their room, bathing, homework, etc. Age-appropriate independent functioning gives a child a feeling of competence and control over his surroundings. This can help the child feel more able to function in school and have the confidence and courage to take steps toward speech.

10. Language issues in bilingual families

If your family is bilingual and your child with SM does not speak the local language fluently, this is an issue that is usually most effectively worked on at home where the child is most relaxed. For a shy child who does not speak in school or kindergarten and is not proficient in the local language, breaking the speech barriers in school in his second, poorly mastered language may prove an insurmountable task. Parents are advised to find ways to encourage their child to speak the local language at home by employing a babysitter or a teenager to engage the child in conversation in the local language in low-pressure, playful activities at home.

Parents may need to consider their attitude toward the local language and attempt to incorporate it more in the home. Many bilingual children with SM express negative attitudes toward the local language, which is a further hurdle to jump over in order to speak freely at school. Here again, parents may decide to try to model more positive attitudes toward the language, perhaps by buying a newspaper or listening to TV channels or radio in the local language. Similarly, immigrant families who maintain a circle of friends who speak their language of origin may try to expand their social network to include those who speak the local language. Parents who are seen by their child to be speaking imperfect English to English-speaking friends in the home can be powerful models their children may be inspired to emulate.

11. Transitions

Starting a new kindergarten or entering first grade may be a stressful experience and, as such, may cause regression if it proves too anxiety provoking for your child. However, a new start can be a window of opportunity for growth. A new teacher with whom the child has not yet established his non-talking behavior can sometimes break the cycle when she implements a behavior modification plan before the school year begins. If the new teacher is prepared to come to the child's home in the summer and carry out the home-based sessions described in the Therapist's Manual (sessions 1-i –1-iv, pages 94-97) and then carry out a school-based session before classes begin (session 2-i, page 99), this may be sufficient to enable the child to speak to the teacher in school or kindergarten once the academic year begins. For a full explanation, read the description of these sessions in the Therapist's Manual.

During any transition from one class to another, the parents should try to ease the child's anxiety by enabling him to become familiar with the new place, teachers, and children before the move occurs. Staff must be made aware of the anxiety issues of the child so that they will attempt to be as sensitive as possible to his needs.

12. Keeping an open mind and a watchful eye

Parents are constants in the childhood and adolescence of their children and are in a position to follow up over time; they will witness pitfalls, transitions, and achievements. It is possible that after the SM has been overcome, your child will have residual anxiety issues that you may want to address. For example, if your child remains excessively shy, cognitive-behavioral techniques could help him gain confidence. Parents must keep an open mind and a watchful eye so that all is done to ensure that their child continues to grow in confidence and social skills over time.

CBT WORKSHEET 1
A basic premise of Cognitive-Behavioral Therapy is that
Thoughts → Feelings → Behavior
Here follows a (very simplified) example:

1. Situation: I see a big dog.

2. Anxious thought: "He might bite me!"

3. Feelings: I am terrified.

4. Behavior: I run for my life.

2. Calm thought: "He's probably harmless."

3. Feelings: I feel fine.

4. Behavior: I continue on my way.

Here we can see how our thoughts affect our feelings, which in turn affect our behavior. If we can learn to channel our thoughts in more productive ways, we can gradually learn to overcome our anxieties.

CBT WORKSHEET 2

Having a child with selective mutism can be anxiety provoking for parents, and if this parental worry is perceived by the child, it can, in turn, make the child with SM more anxious.

The situation is this:
1. My child has selective mutism

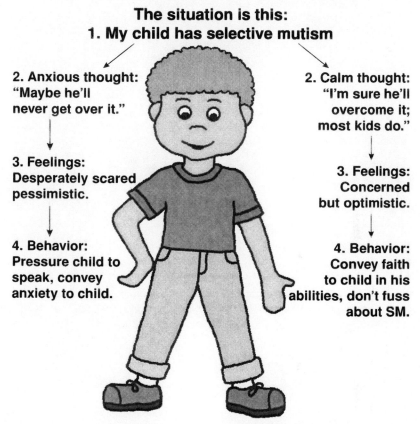

2. Anxious thought:
"Maybe he'll never get over it."

↓

3. Feelings:
Desperately scared pessimistic.

↓

4. Behavior:
Pressure child to speak, convey anxiety to child.

2. Calm thought:
"I'm sure he'll overcome it; most kids do."

↓

3. Feelings:
Concerned but optimistic.

↓

4. Behavior:
Convey faith to child in his abilities, don't fuss about SM.

Children know their parents so well! When we feel despair, our children absorb it and themselves feel more anxious. That is why when there are anxiety issues in the families of children with SM, and parents or siblings learn how to better control their anxiety, it has a ripple effect on the child too.

The Selective Mutism
Treatment Guide

Teacher's Manual

still waters run deep

Contents of Teacher's Manual

Introduction

A challenge and a mystery confront a school or kindergarten teacher when a child fails to speak in her class. She may wonder: Can he speak, does he speak normally at home, why doesn't he speak, what is causing his silence, and is it something personal against me?

Then a host of further questions: How are his language skills, what are his cognitive abilities, how are his social skills, are there problems in his family, has some traumatic event caused his most unusual behavior?

And then still another bout of moot points: Should he be in my class, does he require special education; can I give him what he needs?

And finally, the most dramatic questions of all: Can he break free of his maladaptive silence, what is the treatment of choice, will he respond to the treatment?

Selective mutism often presents as a riddle. However, on further consideration, it is usually less mysterious than it seems. Much is now known about the causes and treatment of selective mutism, and on these pages answers will be given to all the questions posed above (and more…).

Firstly the answer to the last question: a resounding yes! Children with selective mutism usually respond well to the appropriate treatment and break free of their silent shackles in a relatively short-term intervention program. What's more, most of them function normally after they overcome selective mutism. They may remain shy and reticent but within regular parameters. In this manual, you will learn what SM is, how it can be treated, and how you as a teacher are in the eye of this storm, strategically placed exactly where the symptom is usually strongest—in school or kindergarten. In this treatment program, you may be a significant agent of change within a comprehensive program for the treatment of SM.

What Is Selective Mutism?

Selective mutism (SM) is a childhood social communication disorder in which children consistently fail to speak in select situations despite the ability to understand and use language. Children with SM usually speak to family members at home, but do not speak at school. The speech patterns of each child with SM vary along a continuum of severity, from children who speak to everyone outside school and select peers in school, through children who fail to speak to everyone in school, including peers and staff. Some will not speak to anyone outside their home or only to certain family members inside their home, and a rare few do not speak to family members inside the home. Often there is a marked contrast between the outgoing and communicative child at home and the inhibited, introverted functioning at school.

When another condition exists that better accounts for the failure to speak, such as autism, retardation, psychosis, or a lack of language skills, then the child is not considered to have SM.

There are additional traits that have been found in research to be associated with SM; again, each child has a unique set of characteristics. Research studies have found that around 90% of children with SM suffer from social anxiety, and 30–40% have some language or speech impairment. Other associated conditions could include shyness and hypersensitivity, oppositional behavior, stubbornness and perfectionism, and learning disabilities.

There is often a genetic component of shyness or a history of SM in one of the parents or siblings, and sometimes bilingualism or disconnectedness from the cultural milieu of the outside society is found in the families of children with SM.

No link has been found between intelligence and SM, and no link has been found in the large research studies between traumatic events and SM. For a sensitive, anxious child, seemingly everyday events may be experienced as traumatic, such as being shouted at by a teacher, being embarrassed in front of a class, or being mocked by peers for a mispronunciation.

Most research has found that the incidence of SM is around 0.7%, or seven children in every one thousand, and it is three times that number for children from bilingual homes. It is most prevalent between the ages of four and eight. Onset usually occurs when the child first enters an educational framework in which speech is expected, but sometimes onset is gradual—the child's speech output diminishes until he eventually stops speaking.

What Causes Selective Mutism?

Selective mutism is caused by the interaction between the nature of the child and external factors—nature and nurture. One can conceptualize this as various factors fitting into one of three groups: predisposing factors, triggers, and maintaining factors. (Adapted from Shipon-Blum 2007.)

Predisposing factors could include a child who is anxious, shy, hypersensitive or has a family history of shyness, anxiety, or selective mutism. This may include anxious parents and anxious behavior modeling by parents. Other predisposing factors could include speech impairments (usually expressive language), bilingualism, a negative self-image related to speech (e.g. not liking the sound of one's voice), and learning disabilities.

Triggers could include school or kindergarten admission, frequent geographical moves, the child's family belonging to a linguistic minority, or negative reactions to the child talking—bullying, shouting, mocking, etc.

Maintaining factors could include the following: the social isolation of families, misdiagnosis (that is, the child is wrongly diagnosed as having oppositional behavior, autism, retardation, etc.), or a lack of early and appropriate intervention. Other maintaining factors could be the lack of understanding by teachers, families, and psychologists; reinforcement of the mutism by increased attention or affection; heightened anxiety levels caused by pressure to speak; the ability to convey messages nonverbally; a lack of belief by significant adults in the child's ability to overcome the selective mutism.

When there is a combination of predisposing factors that heighten the child's vulnerability to SM, and triggers—events such as kindergarten admission or a geographical move—the scales could tip and bring about the onset of SM.

How Does Selective Mutism Present in School?

As explained above, each child with SM has his own configuration of where and with whom he doesn't speak. Some will not talk to anyone in school, while others will talk to staff and not to peers, and yet others will talk to friends and not to teachers. Many children with SM will whisper to one or two friends who become their spokespersons to the rest of the school. Some children will fully participate in all school activities except for those requiring speech, and some will participate in few activities. Some are very communicative using nonverbal gestures and facial expressions, while others may barely communicate nonverbally and may seem to be wearing a mask devoid of facial expression. Some children with SM may have a vibrant social life, while others may be socially isolated. At the end of the spectrum of severity of SM are children who appear frozen—they may not move unless guided by the teacher, nor eat, nor go to the bathroom. These children are often misdiagnosed as being autistic because that appears to be the case based on their behavior in school.

How does it affect the teacher?
A child with SM is often unobtrusive and undisruptive in the class. He will not be found to upturn tables or talk out of turn. This is why SM frequently remains undiagnosed and untreated—sometimes even unnoticed for many years. But for a teacher who strives to involve her students in class discussions and wishes to get to know the children and to further their academic and social development, a child with SM can be disconcerting. Furthermore, the implementation of what for many teachers is the intuitively obvious way to treat selective mutism— persuading the child to speak by using positive and negative methods (prizes or punishments)—can make things worse and rarely improves matters. It can be frustrating for teachers and it can feel personal, as if the teacher has done something wrong, when a child will not verbally respond to her. This is why it is usually necessary for a teacher to receive guidance on how to understand and help a child with SM.

Understanding the Child with Selective Mutism

While each child with SM has a unique configuration of functioning and emotions, certain reactions and feelings are common. One thing is almost always the case with a child who is not speaking in kindergarten or school: a child with SM suffers! He cannot be himself—the more spontaneous, communicative child he is in other contexts. He must expend effort to ensure that his radar informing him of who is in his proximity is always on, and control himself so that when his private space is encroached, or when he is in a setting in which he does not speak, he stays quiet. High and constant energy expenditure is required to maintain this awareness and control. This in itself is anxiety producing, however effortless the child with SM makes it appear.

The lack of verbal communication causes the child to miss out on social and learning experiences which would further his development. A child who cannot say what he wants will frequently be included in activities he wishes to avoid and conversely will be excluded from experiences he desperately wants to have. This is a recipe for frustration. This frustration is often taken out on his family when he returns home and can finally express himself. Sometimes the frustration expresses itself in school as the child makes his presence felt with his hands rather than his voice.

When a child with SM is unfortunate enough to be in a context in which he is misunderstood and considered to be unintelligent, unable to communicate, or oppositional, he may be inappropriately labeled and consequently placed in an unsuitable learning environment. This frequently exacerbates the child's difficulties. Parents confronted with a child who fails to speak in school frequently go through a period of heightened anxiety themselves. The parents' concern for their child and their grappling with schools and possible interventions as well as long-term projections and postulations regarding future implications for their beloved child can be overwhelming. To make matters worse, the parents' posturing to get appropriate intervention for their child can be misconstrued as over protectiveness and identified by the school as the cause, not the effect, of the child's SM.

For all these reasons (and many more), early intervention is vital. What's more, it usually works! Response to intervention using behavioral therapies for children with SM has been found to be highly effective. In addition, the following treatment plan is generally experienced by the child as an enjoyable, satisfying experience. Once children break the barriers and speak, they usually experience a surge of self-confidence.

How to Treat Selective Mutism

It is widely accepted today that behavioral methods with cognitive components are usually the most effective way to treat SM. It is also known that SM is usually anxiety-based, and that the family and school should be intimately involved in any course of treatment. In order for this to happen, it is vital to establish an open, communicative, and mutually respectful relationship between the teacher, the parents, and the therapist.

This treatment program aims to build bridges between the diverse settings in which the child lives, enabling him to move more confidently between the home and school. In other words, it aims to understand what allows him to speak at home and to try to incorporate those elements at school so that he will feel more comfortable there. At the same time, some factors at school may be conducive to assertiveness and independence, and the parents may wish to incorporate these factors at some level at home. This outlook is reflected in the locations of the therapy—at home and at school, as will be seen below.

This manual is presented as a part of a comprehensive treatment plan for therapist, parents, and teacher, each with their own tasks but working in conjunction with each other. This is in an ideal situation where there are the resources and the will to tackle SM from all three directions. However, if a full-scale intervention is not possible or it is thought that it is not called for, then this treatment plan offers a variety of ideas, interventions, and activities that can be implemented by the teacher, the parents, and the therapist alone without the full-scale program. In many cases, a partial implementation of the program can bring desirable results; often it is sufficient to help the child overcome selective mutism.

Overview of Therapy

The therapy plan before you employs behavioral methods and aims to **remove the symptom of failure to speak** in certain settings. I believe that, especially with young children, symptom removal is paramount because the symptom can affect the child's natural social, speech, and learning development as well as exerting a powerful influence on how the child feels about himself—his self-confidence, his social self-image, and his view of himself as "normal." In addition to this aim of facilitating speech, during the assessment stage other issues may have been found that can be addressed within this therapy, such as independence, assertiveness, and anxiety within the family. These may be incorporated as aims within the therapy, as part of the parents', teacher's, and therapist's interventions.

In some cases, children with SM have additional difficulties other than failure to speak. Some have speech impediments, and others may have additional anxiety issues that may require specific treatment beyond the scope of this plan. Once the non-speech is remedied, the child will be more able to participate in the requisite treatment for other difficulties should they exist.

When a child successfully overcomes SM, this in itself has a powerful self-affirming effect. The child learns that he has the courage to overcome difficulties, and this can have a ripple effect on further problems the child may have, especially anxiety-related issues.

Prior to the start of treatment, the therapist should interview the parents and the teacher in order to assess the child's speech patterns, his strengths and difficulties, and other factors relating to SM. After the assessment is completed, therapy sessions with the child may begin while guidance is given simultaneously to the teacher and the parents. The therapist will explain the therapy outline to the parents and will give ongoing updates regarding progress once therapy has started. Three-way meetings involving the therapist, school staff, and parents should be held at regular intervals.

Here follows a summary of the therapist's sessions with the child, then the parents' interventions will be outlined, and then I will focus on what you as a teacher can do to help the child to overcome SM in school.

The Stages of Therapy: Home-Based, School-Based

A primary aim of the therapy is to build on the child's optimum functioning, which is usually at the home, and to facilitate similar behavior in other surroundings. As such, the **therapy begins, whenever possible, at home**. The aim of these home sessions is to reach the stage wherein the child speaks directly and comfortably to the therapist.

In the initial sessions in the child's home, the therapist will engage in minimal small talk with the parent, trying to be unobtrusive to the child. The initial aim is that the child will talk in the presence of the therapist. Gradually over the course of the home sessions, the therapist will play with the child and other family members and will finally direct speech to the child and play alone with him. By the end of the home sessions stage of the program, the child should be speaking directly with the therapist.

In the final home session, the therapist explains to the child that she works with children in schools, and that she intends to have sessions with the child in school in the coming weeks. In these sessions she will play with the child, sometimes together with other children, and hopefully help him to feel comfortable and enjoy school. (With older children, a more cognitive-behavioral method is used, and there is open discussion about the failure to speak as outlined in Appendix 2, page 118, of the Therapist's Manual. With children up to around third grade, a more behavioral approach is usually recommended.)

Once the child speaks to the therapist in the home, the **therapy is moved to the school**. Therapy will take place one to three times a week in a designated room in the school. Initially, the aim of the sessions will be for the child to speak to the therapist in the room in school. Activities will include games conducive to speech, listening to recordings of the child from home, and arts and crafts. The activities included in these sessions will be modified in accordance with the child's preferences.

Usually this transfer of location goes smoothly, and the child continues to speak to the therapist in the school-based therapy room. Sometimes the child is reticent to speak in the new school setting. If this is the case, the therapist will employ a variety of tools to facilitate speech. This could include recording the child at home and playing the tape in the sessions, including a sibling or inviting the parents to participate in the initial school sessions. There are also behavioral tools that can be used, such as the "sliding in" technique, a form of stimulus shaping developed by Johnson and Wintgens (2001). Here the parent is alone with the child in the room in school, and the child speaks to him. Then a game is played involving rote speech and some physical activity; for example, the parent and child throw a ball between them and each time the thrower says a number. In small but sure stages, the therapist gradually comes within hearing range of the game, eventually enters the room, and finally participates in the game. This may take place in one session or may require several, depending on the progress rate of the child.

Once the child is speaking to the therapist in school, **the generalization stage** begins. Here the aim is **to broaden the child's speaking habits** to include as many people as possible, at first within the therapy room at school. The therapist invites classmates and staff to join in the sessions in small steps and employs behavioral techniques when necessary.

Once the child is speaking to several people in the therapy room, the next stage is to broaden the settings in which the child speaks. In order to achieve this, the sessions are moved either to an open space in the school, such as a hall or play area, or to a corner in the class itself. Here, using the same methods of playing, recording, and other activities used up to now, the child is enabled to speak in the classroom setting. Usually, as the child progresses in therapy, simultaneous progress is seen in other settings. For example, when the child starts speaking in the sessions to a number of children, it is likely that he will speak to some of these children in recess or perhaps quietly in the classroom.

Parents' Interventions and Tasks

Here follows a summary of suggested parents' interventions to be carried out in conjunction with the therapist and teacher. For a fuller description of the parents' interventions, see the Parents' Manual.

Assessment: The parents' input is vital at the assessment stage, as they are often the only ones who are witness to their child's optimum speech functioning and have the sensitivity and intuition to consider and select realistic goals and time frames.

Home therapy sessions: The initial therapy sessions take place in the home and are planned and led by both the therapist and the parents.

School therapy sessions: Once the therapy sessions are moved to the school, the parents will help prepare the homework for the sessions, which is often recordings or films of the child, and they may be asked to attend certain school therapy sessions if the child's progress stalls at one of the transitional stages.

School-based talking-playing sessions: Whenever possible, it is recommended that parents go to the child's school or nursery between one and three times a week, for short talking-playing sessions. This will be described in more detail below, as it must be carried out in conjunction with the teacher and at her convenience.

Inviting friends home, telephone calls, recordings: Helping the child speak to peers at home will make it easier for him to begin to speak at school. Even if he fails to speak at home, inviting friends home will help develop his social skills. The teacher can advise parents as to whom she considers to be compatible for home play-dates. Telephone calls may be a first step in verbal communication with schoolmates and staff, and can be encouraged by parents. Recordings are a useful pre-direct speech step where a child's voice is present without him having to speak directly. Parents are recommended to accustom their child to play with voice recordings, which can be useful in school and therapy as described more fully below.

Desensitization outside school: The behavioral techniques that the therapist is using in school may be implemented at home, which will take the child from silence to speech in small structured steps. This could include helping the child to speak to friends or family members at home or helping him to speak in a restaurant or store. The therapist may guide the parents in the construction and application of a behavior modification program. Many parents have successfully implemented such programs independently, expanding their child's circle of friends and relatives with whom they speak.

Lowering anxiety: An underlying premise of the treatment of SM is that it is usually anxiety-based, and in order to free the child of SM, effort must be made in all settings to lower the child's anxiety levels. Parents learn to ease the pressure on their child to speak, minimizing or eradicating both positive and negative reinforcements, both of which may make the child more anxious about his SM.

Modeling: Research has found that often (but not always) one of the parents of a child with SM has some anxiety issues himself, and in these cases parents are encouraged to attempt to model overcoming their anxieties and broadening their social circles. When parents feel that this is relevant and desirable, they may receive guidance from the therapist on how to foster and model brave, outgoing behavior to their children.

Increasing independence: Parents are encouraged to consider how to increase their child's independence and feelings of competence at home, which will fortify their self-confidence and school functioning.

Bilingual children and immigrants: Bilingual children who are not confident in English should receive informal, playful language tutoring at home where they are more verbal and less anxious. For a timid child, overcoming selective mutism in a language in which he feels incompetent could be an insurmountable challenge.

Teachers' Interventions and Tasks

The teacher is a pivotal player in any attempt to ease the child's selective mutism because in almost all cases, the symptom—failure to speak—is at its strongest in her area of jurisdiction. It is also here in school that much of the fallout from the SM occurs. Apart from the constant self-control, frustration, and suffering that a child experiences having to maintain his silence day in day out for hours at a stretch, further negative side effects occur.

The child may perceive himself to be different and less competent than other children, having failed to master a basic communication tool in school. This may cause the child to develop a negative self-image, which may linger long after the SM is gone. It requires great sensitivity on the part of the teacher to convey to the child belief in his abilities and potential that goes so far beyond the narrow area of difficulty speaking in school.

The specific tasks that teachers can carry out in order to assist the child in his struggle to overcome SM fall into six general areas:

1. Developing a communicative relationship between the teacher and child

Often when confronted with a child with SM, the teacher feels that the basic key to communication is missing, so that a personal relationship between her and the child is not feasible. This attitude, while understandable, is not only misguided, it is damaging to the child. Usually a child with SM is very sensitive, and he cannot tell you or others with words the numerous things that may be upsetting him in the course of a school day. So for this child, even more than for others, a personal relationship with the teacher is vital in order to ease his troubled school experience. It is also his very communication impediment that can be improved by a personal relationship with the teacher, whereby he may gain the invaluable experience of a close relationship with an adult in school. This is a building block toward speech; as he becomes comfortable communicating nonverbally with the teacher and feels the positive effects on his school experience, his anxiety will decrease and he may feel braver in his attempts to talk.

But how can one build a communicative relationship with a child who doesn't talk? Indeed, it is not simple and calls for sensitivity, resourcefulness, creativity, persistence, and most of all, patience. The teacher must **set aside a five-minute slot every day** if possible, otherwise at least three times a week during which she will try to build a communicative, reciprocal relationship with the child. I know that this alone is a lot to ask of a teacher of a large bustling class. But usually this investment of the teacher's time generates ample dividends. The sessions should be pleasant, unpressured, and designed not to raise the anxiety level of the child. Initially, depending on the severity of the SM, the child may barely respond. Take as a starting baseline whatever nonverbal communication the child is able to convey. This may be nodding, pointing, smiling, or eye contact. Build the initial sessions on questions that will not be alarming for the child but will show that you are interested in him and want to get to know him. These reticent children may take a few seconds longer to respond than is common in most conversations. Be sure to wait those extra seconds and not to go on to the next question! Show him that you believe in his ability to communicate to you by giving him that extra time to respond. **Children usually perceive our belief in them, and this bolsters their belief in themselves**. Be sure not to expect or demand responses from the child that are beyond his current ability. For example, do not demand a verbal answer if the child is not able to talk in school, or pointing if the child barely nods his head.

51

When the child perceives your care and investment in him, he may feel more at ease and able to broaden his communications repertoire and you might discuss issues that could improve his school experience. For example, you could ascertain if he is happy sitting in his place in the class or being part of a certain reading group, or if he would like to participate in a certain project. In this way, he will deepen his connection to you and also see that he stands to gain from his communication in that it may solve some of his problems in school. This serves a double purpose. He is simultaneously experiencing a supportive, pleasant, communicative relationship with a teacher, and through it he is finding solutions to his difficulties. This will give him a taste of how much easier life will be once he can talk.

Finally, this personal relationship will be the sheltered cocoon in which the teacher may implement a behavior modification schedule enabling direct speech between the child and herself, as described below.

2. The teacher's behavior modification plan

A behavioral treatment schedule, in many ways similar to that implemented by the therapist in her sessions, may be constructed for you to use in class. The aim would be to build on whatever communication the child is initially able to employ with you, and take small controlled steps toward speech. It may be helpful to start with a couple of home visits, perhaps the child will speak in your presence or to you at home. Even if he doesn't, it will show your interest in him, and slightly blur the boundaries between home and school. See point 6 below for more on home visits. The school sessions should be planned together with the therapist and parents. To this end it is important to **hold regular sessions, a few times a week**—a daunting task for a teacher of a large and lively class, but a key to steady progress.

The first step would be to build a reciprocal, communicative, pleasant relationship, as described in point 1 above. In the framework of this relationship, you could gradually work toward broader nonverbal communication, such as pointing, gestures for "like" and "dislike," and so on. Then you could try to utilize recordings. Using a small office tape recorder, you could ask a few easy questions, like what is your favorite color or how many siblings do you have, and then ask the child to record the answer at home and play it to you in your next session. Or it may be easier for the child to record himself reading at home and to play it to you in school. Once the child is playing recordings of himself reading to the teacher comfortably in school, the teacher may ask the child to read one of the sentences she has just heard on the tape. When listening at school to recordings made at home, it is vital that it takes place initially in a private room, so that the child will not be heard by all his classmates to begin with. If this is successfully carried out over a few sessions, the place at which the teacher hears the recordings could be changed to a more public area, perhaps a corridor, and eventually it could be next to the teacher's desk in the class. This should be done with great sensitivity, ensuring that each change is neither too early, nor too anxiety provoking for the child. The rule of slow but sure progress will allow each step to be within the child's bearable anxiety zone.

If no therapist is involved in the care of the child and available to guide you in the construction and application of a behavior modification program, then you could read the Therapist's Manual (pages 92-115) and adapt sessions within it to be carried out by you or another staff member in school. The sessions are designed to guide the child gently from cooperation, to nonverbal communication, and ultimately to verbal communication using behavioral techniques. These sessions could include the child's parents as well as peers with whom the child speaks outside school (if such exist). It is important to read the Therapist's Manual thoroughly before implementing a treatment plan so that you will understand the basic premises that greatly facilitate progress, such as gradual progression and short, enjoyable sessions.

Teacher-therapist mini-coaching conversations: I have found it most effective to coach the teachers who are carrying out a behavior modification plan with a child, by building a structured intervention plan which is depicted in a chart, and having brief phone conversations with the teacher after each of her sessions. In these mini-coaching conversations we consider together the appropriateness of the goal set for the child in the recent session, the child's response, and plan together what to aim for in the upcoming teacher-child session. In a teacher's pressured and busy schedule, these 5 minute coaching\evaluating\planning phone calls with a therapist following each teacher-child session, keep up momentum, involvement and commitment. It encourages the teacher to be consistent in carrying out regular, scheduled, pre-planned sessions and keeps progress on track.

Table 1 on the following page: **Example of a stepladder of goals for a teacher's behavior modification schedule: five minute sessions held by Ms. Clarke and Liz in kindergarten,** is simplified and concise, and in all probability some of the stages would be repeated a number of times in order to be consolidated before moving on to the next goal. In addition, although it is omitted for the sake of readability and simplicity, in every session, before attempting a new goal, **previously accomplished tasks are repeated before the new behavior goal is attempted.** Obviously, this is just an example, to give flesh to the idea of a teacher's behavior modification plan; for each child a tailor made plan would have to be built, based on his baseline of current communication in school, his strengths and difficulties. The program would have to be fine tuned and altered depending on how the child responds to each attempted goal.

As mentioned above, it is based on the principles outlined in the Therapist's Manual, which should be read before embarking on any treatment schedule.

Table 1: Example of a stepladder of goals for a teacher's behavior modification schedule.

Five minute sessions held by Ms. Clarke and Liz in kindergarten.

Ladder of tasks Session #	Mini-coaching phone call with therapist after session	Result-Date
1. Ms. Clarke engages Liz in conversation in private room, Liz answers Ms. C.'s questions by nodding yes and no.	10.12.2011	Liz nodded yes\no 10.12.2011
2. Ms. C. asks what Liz likes to eat, Liz points to pictures of food in a book in response.		
3. Liz plays a pre-recorded tape of her saying a phrase of a nursery rhyme, (looking at a storybook depicting the rhyme) to Ms. C.		
4. Liz plays a pre-recorded tape of her saying a phrase of a nursery rhyme to Ms. C. then says the same sentence to Ms. C. directly.		
5. Liz plays Chinese whispers with Ms. C. and Joan (Liz speaks to Joan outside school and whispers to her in school).		

Ladder of tasks Session #	Mini-coaching phone call with therapist after session	Result-Date
6. Liz plays hot\cold with Ms. C. and Joan, whispering hot\cold into a microphone.		
7. Liz, Joan, Ms. C. play "snap", Liz says "snap" when 2 cards are identical.		
8. Liz, Joan and Ms. C. play 20 questions, Liz answers yes and no to the questions.		
9. Liz, Joan and Ms. C. play " I went to the store and bought a....." each player adding an item in turn.		
10. Session 9 is repeated in a public space in the kindergarten when the other children are in the yard.		
11. Session 9 is repeated in the public area inside the kindergarten when other children are in the room.		

3. Lowering the child's anxiety level in school

As previously explained, SM is usually an anxiety-based condition. In the past, this sensitive child's response to an anxiety-provoking experience was to refrain from talking. This may have happened on the first day of a new kindergarten, or when shouted at, or when he felt insecure in his language or social skills, or when asked a question he felt uncomfortable answering. Since then the selective mutism has become ingrained in how he responds (or fails to do so) in some situations.

In order to establish conditions conducive to starting to talk, steps should be taken to lower the child's anxiety in school. The **personal contact with the teache**r described above is a big step toward making the child more comfortable in school. Other steps can be considered within the framework of this teacher-child communicative relationship. Often children with SM find themselves sitting next to incompatible peers and have no way to express their distress. Try to find out **whom the child would be happiest sitting next to, as well as at which place in the class**—perhaps not right in the front where he is in the limelight and under the constant scrutiny of teachers. Similarly in kindergarten, at circle time, there may be children next to whom the child suffers, unnoticed.

A main way to lower the child's anxiety in school or kindergarten is to **refrain from putting pressure on the child to speak** when he is not ready to do so. Often in their enthusiasm to get the child talking, teachers feel intuitively that some coaxing in that direction would suffice to get him to speak. In fact, the opposite is nearly always the case. The less pressure is put on the child to talk, the lower his anxiety levels will drop, and the more comfortable he will be. Once he feels at ease, he will be closer to being confident enough to speak.

Pressure to speak can take two forms: positive and negative. Neither is generally productive. Positive pressure can be the promise of a prize or a candy if a child says "good morning," and negative pressure could be not allowing a child to participate in an activity or receive a candy if he fails to answer a question. In many kindergartens, the teacher may ask the child to speak to her every morning for an entire year, is disappointed time and again, and the result is that every morning on entering the kindergarten the child is asked to do something that he is unable to do. That surely is an anxiety-provoking start (or middle, or end) to the child's day. Within the behavior-shaping program described here, small, structured, non-anxiety-provoking steps can be taken by the teacher to guide the child gently toward speech.

Schools and kindergartens abound with other potentially anxiety-provoking activities for a sensitive child in addition to speaking. Care should be taken to allow the child with SM to modify or circumvent these tasks. Here again, all rests on the personal relationship between the teacher and child, which enables the teacher to understand what exactly the child perceives as anxiety provoking. This could include (and varies for each child) writing on the board, participating in plays and dances, leading the children out to recess, and giving out papers to the other children, to name just a few. Here there is a very fine line between respecting the child's nature by not asking him to do something that is too difficult for him, and **encouraging him to participate as fully as possible in kindergarten or school.** It requires great discernment on the part of the teacher to perceive where that line lies. While not wanting to cause the child anxiety, you want to involve him in school activities as much as he is able to do so within his comfort zone and work toward expanding his social and academic participation in school.

A final point under the category of lowering the child's anxiety is the **way in which you talk about the child's selective mutism**, both to the child himself, and to the other children in his class. The two keys are **normalization** and a **calm, optimistic** take on SM. When children ask, "Why doesn't Jenny speak?" your answer should be along the lines of "Jenny does speak perfectly at home, and I'm certain that she will speak here soon as well." In your words and tone you are showing the children that it is not so pathological—Jenny does speak at home— nor such cause for concern, as you have confidence in Jenny that she will overcome the SM. Once again, your belief in the child's ability to progress is a potent force for strengthening her self-confidence and belief in her ability to develop and overcome.

The same elements should shape the way you talk to the child about his selective mutism. This should seldom be discussed unless the subject is initiated by the child or it is decided otherwise in a broad therapy intervention plan. If your understanding of the child's SM is reiterated too often, this in itself can become a form of pressure. Your message should be: **"There are many children who find it difficult to talk in school who do manage to talk after a while [normalization], we know how to help you [the child is not alone in his struggle], and I am sure you will overcome it soon [confidence and belief in the child's strengths]."** In this way, the child learns that many other children also have SM, that it can be and usually is overcome, that you have confidence in his ability to speak normally, and that you can help him in his quest to speak.

4. Facilitating social interaction with other children

A child who does not speak in kindergarten or school will lose valuable communication and social skills experience. Depending on the form the SM takes, the child may be social and involved in reciprocal relationships with peers in ways other than speech, or he may be withdrawn and isolated. In all cases, the teacher's gentle intervention to enable maximum social interaction is recommended.

With a withdrawn child, the teacher should consider who may be compatible playmates and try to couple the child with SM together with those children. This could be in free play, in the seating place in the room, or in small groups. If you have developed a personal relationship with the child, you may be able to facilitate this social interaction by being a part of the small group initially until the child feels at ease without you by his side.

5. Building independence, assertiveness, and self-esteem in school

Selective mutism can infuse some children with a desperate sense of lack of control; they have lost the usual means children have of controlling their surroundings with their speech, such as requesting certain foods or social and academic activities, as well as voicing their unwillingness to be part of other goings-on with peers and in their studies. Again, the degree to which this sense of lack of control occurs varies from child to child, but it is intrinsic in the failure to speak of selective mutism. Teachers should attempt to return some control to the child by structuring the child's human and learning environment.

The first way this can be done is by **maximizing any communication abilities the child has;** if he can communicate by gestures, use these to the hilt. Involve him in choices; ask his opinion in a way he will be able to respond with the gestures in his repertoire. Construct further nonverbal gestures to enable him to convey to you common needs, such as going to the bathroom, feeling hungry, wishing to go to the yard, and so on. Use your creativity to find ways to give him a say in what he does. Encourage him to be assertive, both in the academic and the social choices he makes.

Consider what his strengths are and try to highlight these to fortify his self-esteem. Many children with SM develop alternative ways of reaching out to others, such as music and art. If this is the case with your student, give him a position in class that will make these abilities prominent and appreciated without intimidating the child by putting him in the limelight more than his comfort level allows. He may possess academic strengths; make sure other children are aware of his abilities and that he is made to feel really good about them. You could praise his work, frame and display it, read out his essays, or show his Lego construction, for example. In short, show him that you think him able and esteemed for who he is and what he does.

A powerful, insidious force at work in the relationship between the child and his teacher is her **belief (or lack of it) in the child**— his strengths, his personality and skills, and his ability to overcome his selective mutism. Teachers often feel hopeless, helpless, and desperate when considering the prospects of a child with SM. It may be hard to understand how a child who does not speak, contrary to all normal behavior and expectations and despite incessant cajoling and persuading, will be able to start speaking in school. Children perceive what you think and expect of them, and they may be convinced by a teacher's pessimism and feel hopeless themselves as a result. In stark contrast, a teacher's belief in a child's ability to overcome will be perceived by the child and strengthen his feelings of competence and his belief in himself.

A teacher's belief in a child is a powerful force indeed, with tangible, positive effects. But how can you conjure up this belief when it doesn't exist? Here the parents and therapist may come to your aid. From the parents you can hear about the child's ability to speak at home, to converse, argue, sing, and shout. Watch home movies of the child talking, and you will understand that this is who he is when freed from the shackles of his SM. From the therapist—and from me in my experience—you can learn that nearly all children with SM do overcome it in time, and with appropriate help this can be a fairly short process. You have no reason for pessimism, and good reason for optimism. If you let your newfound belief in the child shine through, you will buffer his self-belief and consequently help him to speak in school.

Sometimes it is tempting to "baby" a child with selective mutism. Because he does not speak, his teacher and friends respond for him. Often he would have given an answer through gestures, but those around him did not wait the couple of seconds more he required to give his response. **Return to him the responsibility to respond and make choices in any way he is able,** including gestures, such as nodding, pointing, and using previously decided upon signs.

Similarly, ensure that he is encouraged to be as independent as he can be. Lack of speech is generally no reason to exempt a child from hanging up his coat, unpacking his lunch box, or washing his hands. In extreme cases, selective mutism can present as a child who seems "frozen" and indeed needs help to take out his lunch box. But most children with SM are capable of some level of independent behavior if the staff controls the urge to coddle them. When a child sees himself engaging in independent functioning In school or kindergarten, this fosters within him a feeling of competence and self-esteem.

A word of caution about encouraging writing in place of speaking: It is tempting to use the written word once the child has mastered writing, as a way of communicating things beyond the scope of gestures. I am generally against using written communication for three reasons. It is far removed from verbal and body language, it is not a precursor to speech in the way that gestures are, and it can become entrenched as a good enough way of conveying thoughts and wishes, which may diminish the urgency of acquiring speech in school. However, every teacher must consider for herself the costs and benefits of encouraging written communication in the place of speech for each child.

6. Blurring the distinction between home and school functioning

For the child with selective mutism, school or kindergarten has usually been singled out as the place in which he does not talk, and home as the place in which he does. One of the aims of the intervention is to enable social communication and speech that is closer to the child's home functioning than his current behavior in school. This can be done in two main ways. Firstly, in your open, ongoing meetings and calls with the parents, try to learn what you can do to emulate certain aspects of the home environment in school. The **personal sessions with the child** described above are one way of building a caring, warm relationship in which you attempt to become closer to and more aware of the emotional needs of the child. This may resemble aspects of a close mother-child relationship as contrasted with a more distant teacher-child one. If a child uses email, you could supplement this contact by emailing and receiving emails from him when he is at home. Similarly, if he will speak on the phone, that could be a good way to start verbal contact when he is in the lower-anxiety surroundings of his home.

A second way, which is also a wonderful way to establish a trusting, personal relationship with the parents, is home visits. It shows the child how interested you are in getting to know him and takes you away from being associated exclusively with school. This may take the relationship to a further level of closeness. When visiting at his home, you should not demand any behavior the child has not shown at school—there should be no pressure to speak—but do show interest in his games and hobbies. He can show you his bedroom, yard, computer games he enjoys playing, and so on. You could also play with him a game of his choice. Do not insist on anything that the child shows resistance to doing. See if he is willing to show you a film of him talking without making any fuss on your part of the fact that he is talking. It could be a film of a vacation or some special family activity or birthday. In this way, in a light and pleasant atmosphere, you may hear his voice for the first time! If so, it will be most helpful to continue using the recordings in school, as is described in point 7 below. The visit must be planned together with his parents beforehand so that they will have a film of the child and a game to play at hand, and so that they will understand that no pressure will be placed (by you or them) on the child to speak. A general rule with children who are anxious is not to make too much of a fuss, not to put them in the limelight, not to express too much excitement about their achievements and attributes, as this hullabaloo could increase their feelings of anxiety. So when you do hear the child speak for the first time, be moderately pleased about it, as too much excitement may make him decide to stop talking!

7. Transitions and home visits

When a child moves from one educational setting to another—for example from one kindergarten to another, from kindergarten to school or from one grade to another—this may offer a window of opportunity for change and progress, or conversely it may be stressful and cause regression. Sometimes a fresh start with staff and children who do not have preconceived notions about whether the child speaks, enables him to begin to speak without causing a huge commotion of surprise and excitement among friends and teachers; commotion is usually anathema for an anxious or shy child. However, the opposite may be the case, as an unknown environment and the adjustment it entails may engender higher levels of anxiety and stress, causing the child to retreat further from social communication in school. Therefore, transitions must be approached with caution and sensitivity.

How then, to promote growth during transitions? **Home visits** by an as yet unfamiliar teacher may work wonders. The teacher should visit the home before the school year has begun; she has not yet been associated with school, and she is not yet necessarily included in the group of people with whom the child doesn't speak. The aim of the home visits initially is to hear the child's voice; then engage in some activity in which he speaks, though not directly to the teacher; and finally, engage in direct verbal communication with him. This may occur in one visit or it may (and usually does) take a few visits. The rule is to go slowly in order to enable the child to gradually feel comfortable enough to speak in the presence of a stranger. These home visits are similar to the initial home-based therapy sessions described in the Therapist's Manual, which you may want to read before embarking on this project (pages 94-97).

Home visits must be planned carefully with the parents beforehand so that the teacher may slip into the home environment without fuss and without her focusing on the child in any way. The parents and teacher must plan to ensure that the child will be engaged in an enjoyable activity that requires speech and that takes place in the presence of the teacher.

During the initial home visit, the teacher should aim to be as unobtrusive as possible, a fly on the wall, enabling the child to speak in her presence. There should be no eye contact with the child, no initiation of any communication with the child; she should sit in an unobtrusive place and may engage in minimal small talk with the mother or father. In the Parents' Manual, parents are encouraged to record their child in a playful way for fun. They could play one of these recordings in the initial home visit as long as it is something that they have done before and won't be perceived by the child as something out of the ordinary. In this way, the child's voice would be present from the start. Once the child speaks in the teacher's presence, the next step would be to play a game with the child and another family member in which speech is required, but not direct speech between the child and the teacher. After this has been achieved, the teacher may try to have a direct conversation with the child, again, with sensitivity and gentleness. Finally, once the child is speaking to the teacher at home, one session between the teacher and the child should be held in the kindergarten or school, prior to the beginning of the school year, in which the child talks to the teacher while engaged in activities previously played in the home sessions.

This progression during the home visits from listening to recorded speech, to hearing the child speak, to direct speech with the teacher, usually takes a few sessions, and many teachers may not be available to invest so much time. In that case, one home visit will have to suffice. It should be noted, however, that when a teacher can take the time to go the child's home several times with a pre-planned strategy, it often circumvents months of working toward speech later on in school.

In addition to the teacher's home visits, the parents should be given a list of the children in the new class and encouraged to arrange play-dates so that the child knows some classmates on the first day of school.

Great sensitivity is required by the staff on the initial days of school or kindergarten so that all elements that may make the child less anxious and more confident will be in place. These include sitting him next to a friend and explaining to the other teachers the need to be gentle with him. Finally, if the child becomes acquainted with the physical school premises prior to the beginning of school, he will feel more confident navigating the logistics of getting to his room on the first day.

8. How to slot in with the three-pronged intervention: therapist, parents, teacher — facilitating progress on all three fronts

As has been mentioned, fluid, open, and respectful contact between the school, the parents, and the therapist (in cases in which therapy is taking place) is most conducive to improvement. These three partners must share updates regularly so that the interventions of each side will complement progress on the other fronts. For example, if the parents report that the child is having successful play-dates with a certain classmate, it may be wise for the teacher to sit them together in class.

Once the therapy reaches the stage of school sessions, the therapist will have to coordinate with you in order to set a convenient time and place. At certain points in the school-based sessions, the therapist may wish to invite you to participate in order to generalize the child's speaking in school to include you. At a later stage, sessions will take place within the class, which must also be arranged with you.

Parental playing-talking sessions: It is recommended that parents come to school or kindergarten between one and three times a week for talking-playing sessions. These must be planned by the teacher and parent with the therapist's guidance to ensure that they will take place at a time and location that is convenient for the school. Playing-talking sessions are short, informal periods during which the parent plays and talks with the child in school or kindergarten. The parent considers where in the school her child will speak to her, which depends on the severity of the SM. Some children will speak with a parent or family member in a secluded corner of the class while others need the security of a closed room in order to speak.

These sessions significantly boost the effectiveness of the therapy. Instead of the child speaking once a week in school during one hour in therapy with the therapist, he is now speaking several times a week in school—for example, twice with a family member and once with the therapist. In order to maximize the effectiveness of these sessions, they should be planned with the therapist and the teacher so that they appropriately complement the concurrent stages of therapy and classroom functioning. They will be structured according to the same behavioral principles used in the therapist's interventions—initially the child will speak to the parent in a private area, then the circle with whom he speaks will be gradually enlarged to include friends and staff, and finally his speech will be generalized to include additional settings in the school, such as public areas and the classroom. The aim is to enable him to speak to everyone in all settings. You can read more about the playing-talking sessions in the Parents' Manual, page 21.

A warm, sensitive, and committed teacher can make the world of a difference to a child with SM. By implementing the interventions described here, either as part of a broader treatment plan together with a therapist and parents, or in conjunction with the parents alone, teachers can significantly help a child with SM break out of his silence and join the ranks of socially communicative, talking children in kindergarten and school.

The Selective Mutism
Treatment Guide

Therapist's Manual

still waters run deep

Contents of Therapist's Manual

Introduction

Helping a child with selective mutism may seem to be a near impossible task for a therapist: How can you treat a child who does not speak, perhaps will not use body gestures, and may even appear "frozen" during sessions? And say you do manage to break the barriers during sessions in your clinic, and the child speaks and plays with you, are you really helping him, if in his everyday life his difficulty speaking continues unabated?

Selective mutism—the consistent failure to speak in certain settings or to specific people—necessitates a tailor-made treatment, which is usually based on **behavioral or cognitive-behavioral therapy**. The child with SM needs help in order to function normally in his home, school or kindergarten; in other words, a child suffering from SM needs **early intervention aimed at removing the symptom**— the lack of appropriate speech and communication. This symptom removal must take place in the child's natural environment, not in the sterile, disconnected setting of a therapist's office. This calls for some out-of-the-box thought and practice. The approach outlined in this manual is designed with this aim in mind—enabling the child to talk to everyone everywhere. It is largely behavioral treatment with sessions that take place initially at the child's home, and later on in his school.

It is widely agreed that the treatment of choice for SM is usually behavioral or cognitive-behavioral, with **pharmacological** treatment for anxiety supplementing therapy in stubborn or extreme cases. Yet so many children with SM undergo lengthy courses of play therapy, which often does little to assuage their selective mutism beyond the therapist's office. In practice, the whole range of psychological treatments is used for SM—family, speech, art, music and play therapy, to name a few.

While not denying the place of these and many other therapies, for young children the symptom of not speaking in school or kindergarten is often debilitating. Not speaking can become deeply entrenched and may cause or exacerbate numerous other problems, such as a negative self-image (feeling different and inadequate), social interaction difficulties caused by insufficient practice and exposure to social situations, delayed expressive language development, and a generalized anxiety disorder.

Therefore, therapy that is mainly behavioral with cognitive components (for older and more introspective children, more cognitive elements are included) is usually the preferred treatment. The aim of the therapy is to enable the child to function on a normative level: speak when speech is required, be able to answer adults and peers, and initiate speech with peers. Once this is achieved, there may be residual issues that require further treatment. These may be addressed more effectively once the child will be able to speak in therapy. The importance of early symptom removal is paramount, as it may limit malfunction in related areas (behavior, social skills, etc.) while the acquisition of normative speech will have an immensely powerful effect on the child and his environment, pulling him toward improved functioning in other areas.

This treatment plan is mostly behavioral, yet the process of therapy has numerous **dynamic characteristics** that must be implemented for treatment to succeed. The therapist must have those stalwarts of psychodynamic practitioners—empathy and listening skills—that enable her to build a warm and caring relationship with the child, the soil needed to nurture therapeutic improvement. Due to the sensitive, anxious nature of most children with SM, the therapist must be cautious not to overwhelm the child—to respect the child's shy nature and to communicate and express warmth and encouragement in a way that will not raise the child's anxiety levels.

It is vital to **include the child's parents and teachers in the treatment**; specific manuals are addressed to them. They should be involved in implementing change in the home and school or kindergarten. They should both be consulted for assessment and insight, and be intimately involved and guided by the therapist regarding ways in which they may facilitate progress. The initial therapy sessions take place in the home whenever possible, and fluid communication between the therapist, parents, and teacher is vital. The aim is to blur the borders between home, school, and outside the home. This approach builds on the child's strengths at home and enables him to generalize them to other contexts, making his experiences in diverse settings more consistent and productive.

Other treatment methods, in which the child is treated in a clinic away from the school, have the implicit problem of transferring any progress that has been made in the clinic so that the child implements that change in school. This rarely happens spontaneously as a result of therapy without employing agents for change within the school itself. Thus, when a child with SM undergoes seemingly successful therapy in a clinic, it may have little impact on the child's speech and social functioning in his life outside the clinic.

There is a perfect fit between the **educational or school psychologist, or the school guidance counselor, and SM treatment** in that the school psychologist is strategically based at the spot where the symptom is (usually) most pronounced. After several initial sessions at the home in which verbal communication develops between the therapist and the child, the psychologist can act as a bridge that allows the child to transport his functional speech from the home to the school, in controlled, structured, graduated steps. Having said this, this treatment program can be implemented by others, including speech therapists and teachers, as well as concerned, capable relatives and friends, who have the requisite understanding and characteristics and are available to hold sessions in the child's home and school.

Definition of Selective Mutism

Selective mutism (SM) is a childhood social communication disorder in which children consistently fail to speak in select situations despite their ability to understand and use language. Children with SM usually speak to family members at home, but do not speak at kindergarten or school. The speech patterns of each child with SM vary along a continuum of severity—from children who speak to everyone outside school and select peers in school, to children who fail to speak to anyone in school, including peers and staff. Some will not speak to anyone outside their home or to only certain family members inside their home. Often there is a marked contrast between the outgoing and communicative child at home and the inhibited, introverted child at school.

When another condition exists that better accounts for the failure to speak, such as PDD, retardation, psychosis, or a lack of language skills, then the child does not have SM.

There are many comorbid constellations of traits that have been found in research to be associated with SM. Again, each child has a unique set of characteristics. Research has found that around 90% of children with SM suffer from social anxiety, and about 30% have some language or speech impairment. Other comorbid conditions could include shyness and hypersensitivity, oppositional behavior, stubbornness and perfectionism, neuro-developmental disorder or delay (often auditory processing delay), and learning disabilities.

There is often a genetic component of shyness or a history of SM in one of the parents or siblings, and bilingualism or disconnectedness from the cultural milieu of the outside society is also sometimes found.

No link has been found between intelligence and SM, and none has been found in the large research studies between traumatic events and SM. For a sensitive, anxious child, seemingly everyday events may be experienced as traumatic—such as being shouted at by a teacher, being embarrassed in front of a class, or being mocked by peers for a mispronunciation.

Most research has found that the incidence of SM is around 0.7%, or seven children in every one thousand, and it is three times that number among children from bilingual homes. It is most prevalent between the ages of four and eight. Onset usually occurs when the child first enters an educational framework in which speech is expected, but sometimes onset is gradual—the child's speech output decreases until he eventually stops speaking.

The DSM IV (see Table 2 for DSM diagnostic criteria) states that SM can be diagnosed after one month during which the child fails to speak, not including the first month at school when his initial reticence is not necessarily the forbearer of SM.

Table 2: DSM IV Diagnostic Criteria
(American Psychiatric Association)

Selective Mutism (formerly Elective Mutism)

A. Consistent failure to speak in specific social situations (in which there is an expectation for speaking, e.g. at school) despite speaking in other situations.

B. The disturbance interferes with educational or occupational achievement or with social communication.

C. The duration of the disturbance is at least one month (not limited to the first month of school).

D. The failure to speak is not due to a lack of knowledge of, or comfort with, the spoken language required in the social situation.

E. The disturbance is not better accounted for by a Communication Disorder (e.g. Stuttering) and does not occur exclusively during the course of a Pervasive Developmental Disorder, Schizophrenia, or other Psychotic Disorder.

Causes

Selective mutism is caused by the interaction between the psychological make up of the child and external factors—nature and nurture. One can conceptualize this as various factors fitting into one of three groups: predisposing factors, triggers, and maintaining factors. (Adapted from Shipon-Blum 2007.)

Predisposing factors:

- Child's anxiety, shyness, timidity, hyper-sensitivity
- Family history of shyness, anxiety, or selective mutism—can include anxious parents, anxious behavior modeling by parents
- Speech impairment of child—usually expressive language
- Bilingualism and disconnectedness from the predominant culture
- Neuro-developmental disorder or delay, often auditory processing disorder

Triggers:

- School or kindergarten admission
- Frequent geographical moves
- Family moving to area with different spoken language
- Negative reactions to child talking—bullying, shouting, mocking etc.

Maintaining factors:

- Misdiagnosis (oppositional behavior, autism, retardation)
- Lack of early and appropriate intervention
- Lack of understanding by teachers, families, psychologists
- Reinforcement by increased attention or affection
- Heightened anxiety levels caused by pressure to speak
- Ability to convey messages nonverbally
- Lack of belief in ability to overcome SM
- Social isolation of families

Assessment

It is important to have an accurate appraisal of the baseline functioning of the child who has SM at the beginning of therapy—this includes his functioning at home, at school, and in other settings. A good starting place for initial assessment is a joint interview with the parents, teacher, and therapist. Unless it can be done discreetly, direct observation of the child with SM by the therapist is not recommended at this time since it is preferable to begin the initial home sessions without having been previously noticed by the child in kindergarten or school.

In the assessment interview, it is important to note the following:

From the parents:
- Speaking habits—in which places and to whom the child speaks. See Appendix 1: "Speaking Checklist" (page 116) for easy Documentation
- Etiology of child's speech and social communication
- Child's temperament and characteristics—may be shy, slow to warm, perfectionist, stubborn, persistent, or oppositional
- Child's social functioning—with peers, adults, family members, strangers
- General background of child—pregnancy, birth, early development, feeding, sleeping, toilet training
- Child's current language competence
- Bilingualism, language spoken at home
- Child's anxiety levels in different contexts
- Education history—age child began nursery, kindergarten, school; his functioning in each framework; learning and cognitive abilities and difficulties; social functioning; fine and gross motor skills
- Family interactions with siblings, parents, wider family

- Attachment to and separation from parents
- Family history of anxiety, SM, shyness, and hypersensitivity
- Social/cultural isolation of family, geographical moves
- Child's interests and hobbies, youth groups, after-school classes
- Other difficulties, concerns
- How parents cope with the SM
- Change in SM over time
- Help and treatment received until now

From the teacher:
- Child's speech patterns in school—to whom and in which contexts he speaks and communicates
- Estimation of child's cognitive and learning abilities (may prove to be inaccurate if the child fails to talk to the teacher)
- Estimation of child's fine and gross motor skills
- Participation in school activities
- Separation issues
- Relationship between teacher and child
- Connection between teacher and child's family
- School bathroom habits
- School eating habits
- Social behavior with peers in class and recess
- Interaction with staff
- Child's attention level
- How the teacher manages the SM
- Intervention within the school
- Any change in SM over time
- Other difficulties or concerns
- Child's strengths and interests

Levels of Selective Mutism

The degree of severity of selective mutism varies from child to child and lies upon a continuum. At one end of the continuum is a child who speaks to no one outside his closest family and even fails to speak to some immediate family members; at the other end may be a child who speaks to everyone—adults and peers—except for his teacher in school. The following division of four levels of SM can be broken down into numerous subdivisions. Furthermore, the same child functions differently in different contexts. The child with the most severe SM in kindergarten may have absolutely normal behavior at home and at his grandparents', whereas a child with mild SM in school may also have mild SM in the presence of any non–nuclear family member. Thus these categorizations are not absolute within the functioning of any real child.

1. The most severe level is of total **non–communication** in the places where the child fails to speak. He barely uses nonverbal communication such as nodding. He may have hardly any facial expression, as though he wears a mask. He may be "frozen" in his body gestures, so that he fails to move with spontaneity and may even have to be physically moved from the standing to sitting position by a teacher or to have a spoon placed in his hand before he begins to eat. These children are frequently misdiagnosed in their kindergarten as autistic, and staff are often amazed when the therapist reports regular age and stage appropriate behavior at home.

2. **Nonverbal communication:** The child communicates nonverbally in the place in which his SM is manifest. He may both respond and initiate nonverbally, or it may be hard for him to initiate. He may use gestures such as nodding yes and no and pointing; use facial expressions such as smiling and frowning; use tape recordings or machines with voice emissions; whisper to a chosen spokesperson, peer, or a family

member who relays the message. The child at this level may participate to a greater or lesser degree in kindergarten or school; some children with SM who communicate nonverbally do absolutely everything in school or kindergarten except speak. They may function well socially and perform in school choirs (without emitting a sound!). Others may be reticent and rarely participate in school activities.

3. **Whispering and emitting sounds:** The child may be able to emit sounds, such as animal sounds, clicking with his tongue, whistling, or pronouncing consonants such as "t" or "s." The child fails to emit words at an appropriate volume, but may whisper select or numerous words.

4. **Verbal communication:** The child says words at an audible volume. He may still be reticent, and this may be gradual— first to select staff or peers and slowly generalizing to more people. Initial verbalizations may be reading from cards, indirect speech, or only select words such as yes and no. Some children, once they break the verbal barrier, speak freely to everyone, as though a dam has been burst.

Planning Therapy

Various points must be considered when planning treatment:

1. **The age of the child.** This manual is aimed primarily for the younger child; see Appendix 2 (page 118) for methods for the management of therapy with older children. Up to the age of about eight, therapy methods are primarily behavioral with some cognitive components. This means that goals and stages built by the therapist in the treatment strategy will be, on the whole, implicit, and not explicitly presented to the

child. When working with an older child, particularly teens, the therapy is more transparent in its goals and methods. The therapist and young person work together to understand causes, emotions, and behaviors, building strategies and goals. Thus for the older child, the treatment is cognitive-behavioral, while for the younger child, the emphasis is put on the behavioral axis. Another way of looking at this is that for the younger child, therapy mainly involves playing games, while for the older child it is mostly about setting goals and finding ways to work toward those goals.

2. **Lowering anxiety.** Following on from the conceptualization of SM as anxiety-based, a twofold main aim of therapy will be to lower the child's experience of anxiety and to build up his emotional armor, strengthening his resistance to anxiety-provoking situations. Discussion of the cognitive understanding of emotions and behavior in SM with the child naturally causes an increase in anxiety—it is necessary and productive with older children, but with younger children is often not helpful and therefore can be largely avoided.

   This twofold aim of adjusting the environment in order to lower the child's anxiety levels therein and increasing the child's coping skills in anxiety provoking situations is a foundation of this therapy. Thus the teachers must consider ways to soften the threatening nature of school for the child with SM (see Teacher's Manual). These are often relatively simple changes to implement, such as explaining to all staff members that he should not be expected to speak and should be treated with sensitivity (not be shouted at), or ensuring that he sits next to a considerate child in the classroom or at circle time.

   Parents must consider ways in which they can diminish the pressure on the child to speak and strengthen both the child's belief in himself and his independent, competent functioning (see Parents' Manual). The message implicit (and when necessary explicit) of all those involved in the child's life should be: "We love and accept you exactly as you are; we know you can speak and believe that soon you will be able to speak everywhere." There should be minimal pressure to speak as this increases anxiety levels and, paradoxically, usually makes it harder for the child to start speaking.

Another important point to remember is that excessive praise or being placed in the limelight may be anxiety provoking for an anxious child. I have seen and heard of many instances in which a child speaks for the first time in school; the staff erupts with excitement and lavishes excessive praise on the child, at which point the child is deterred and stops speaking. A nonchalant, moderately pleased attitude should be adopted as the child takes steps towards speech.

Sometimes a child with SM fails to speak but does not seem socially anxious in other ways. The child may indeed not be socially anxious on the whole, yet he has maintained a maladaptive behavior that he originally took on in order to feel more socially comfortable. For example, a bilingual child who when entering kindergarten spoke English poorly, when assessed in first grade may speak perfectly and exhibit normal levels of social anxiety. Yet he cannot change his previously established silent social mores without intervention. Sometimes such children self-report after therapy that they had been waiting and hoping for a helping hand to pull them out of their self-dug hole.

In very stubborn or extreme cases, anxiety-lowering medication may be considered to supplement therapy. This is usually if the SM has become deeply entrenched and is not responding well to behavioral therapy, or if the child is suffering from generalized or other anxiety disorders as well as SM.

3. **Respecting the child's current comfort level.** Before commencing therapy, the child's baseline of speech and communication functioning, as well as the level of his anxiety in different settings, must be assessed. During therapy these must be constantly appraised so that the therapist can plan realistic goals based on furthering progress within the child's comfort zone.

4. **Small steps—great patience!** Therapy must proceed in small steps where the goals are moved gradually, enabling the child to proceed while keeping his anxiety level manageable. This often is perceived by the therapist and school staff as an unbearably slow pace, while, in fact, it is the only way to proceed—in slow but sure steps. Not more than one variable should be changed from session to session, as explained below.

5. **Short, frequent sessions.** The sessions should take place at least once a week (twice or more is preferable) and should last between half an hour to an hour. When it is possible to conduct an intense intervention, with sessions every day for a number of weeks, the improvement is often striking and swift.

6. **Fun!** The sessions should be enjoyable for the child (and the therapist!) and should cater to the child's tastes and preferences. If he enjoys drawing, building, sports, etc., activities can be built around these preferences.

7. **Activities that lower anxiety levels while pursuing a goal.** When trying to attain a behavioral goal, physical activities or games can lower the intensity and pressure of mastering a new speech goal and therefore facilitate attaining that goal. For example, when the aim of the session is that the child speaks to a classmate for the first time, it is helpful to put it in the framework of a game, such as throwing a ball and saying your name as you throw it. This will be elaborated on below.

8. **Addressing the triggers, predisposing factors, and maintaining factors.** In planning treatment, these factors must be borne in mind, so that they can be included in goals to build long-term coping skills and social communication.

9. **Rewards.** In this program, rewards are conspicuously absent! The rewards intrinsic in improved social communication are such that any other prize pales in comparison, and is rendered redundant. Furthermore, the promise of a prize on the completion of a proposed goal can increase anxiety. Within the framework of a warm therapist-child relationship, praise and smiles are rewards indeed. The therapist can decide for herself whether to give the child a candy or small gift to increase the pleasantness of the sessions. The way rewards can be effectively used with young children is when the rewards are not dependent on reaching a preset aim. Thus after sessions the therapist can give the child a small prize, which he can retroactively correlate to some progress made or some positive behavior in the session. The therapist can discern positive behavior, even when none is strikingly apparent, and reward this behavior. In this way, she will build in the child a feeling and expectation of success and progress.

   With older children and teens, rewards can be incorporated and can indeed be motivating elements within a CBT treatment plan, as described in Appendix 2: Cognitive-Behavioral Techniques for Older Children and Teens, page 118.

10. **Bilingual children and immigrants.** Bilingual children who are not confident in English should receive informal, playful language tutoring at home where they are more verbal and less anxious. For a timid child, overcoming selective mutism in a language in which the child feels incompetent often proves to be an insurmountable challenge. Employing a capable, warm teenager to play with the child twice a week at home in English is one way of arranging informal,

enjoyable language experience. This is discussed further in the Parents' Manual (pages 27-28).

11. **Parent and staff involvement.** This has already been frequently mentioned above, but due to the integral place it occupies in this therapy, it is stressed once more: Parents and educational staff are guided to plan and implement their own custom-built interventions which will be complementary to the therapist's treatment. Their principle aims are to decrease pressure on the child to speak in order to lower anxiety levels, and to take steps to foster social communication and ultimately speech. **It is vital that the therapist reads the manuals for parents and teachers** in order to be fully aware of the tasks they will carry out in the framework of the three-way therapeutic alliance. It is the therapist's job to oversee and coordinate the three parties to ensure that they work together and complement each other. Once a behavioral plan has been built to be implemented by the teacher or parent, the therapist must follow up to ensure that it is being carried out as planned and to assist in fine tuning it based on the child's reactions to it. Often the teacher's behavioral plan requires ongoing supervision to see that it is actually happening – a teacher of a bustling, large class is very likely to find it hard to be consistent in carrying out the intervention, and consistency is a vital ingredient of success in such endeavors. A chart in which the teacher may check each intervention, with a brief description of the child's response, to be emailed to the therapist once a week, may engender greater consistency. Thus the teacher's intervention may be a five minute conversation with the child each day, in which the child initially uses gestures, gradually progresses to taped messages, and eventually uses the spoken word. If she ticks off on a chart on completion of each five minute conversation, to be reviewed with the therapist once a week, it may cause these mini sessions to occur regularly. Often, more intensive coaching of the teacher, including a very brief report and evaluation with

the therapist after each mini-session, is conducive to progress. See the Teacher's Manual, (page 56) for a concrete example of a teacher's behavior modification plan.

12. **Transitions.** While transitions can be stressful, they are also windows of opportunity for change. For example, when moving to a new school, home visits by a teacher before the academic year begins may enable the child to talk to his teacher at home. With careful planning, this may be carried over into the school through further school visits with the new teacher before the school year commences. Utilizing the transition and school vacation may well sidestep months of suffering and therapy by enabling the child to speak to his teacher before school begins. This is described more fully in the Teacher's Manual (pages 65-67).

Three Main Tools of Behavioral Therapy

In addition to the dynamic tools of empathy, listening, building rapport, and a warm, supportive relationship, three main behavioral tools are employed at different stages of the therapy.

1. **Desensitization.** A scale is built of imagined and real nonverbal and verbal communication, and the child gradually passes through the stages until he reaches face-to-face verbal communication. For example, he may first speak on the phone, then in a voice recording device, then in a talking picture frame or album (a photo album in which alongside each photograph a short message can be recorded), then whisper to the teacher, and finally talk directly to the teacher.

2. **Stimulus Fading.** The child's speech is constant, but the setting or the people present to hear his speech change. The child

initially talks to the therapist at home, then in a room in school into which children and adults are gradually introduced. Then the setting may be broadened to facilitate generalization. Thus after the child speaks to the therapist and some friends in the closed therapy room, the little group is removed to the kindergarten shared space or classroom, and the child hopefully continues to speak within the open space. It is vital never to change more than one variable at a time, to ensure that the child is comfortable with the current setting and people before changing, and to make the steps as small as possible to ensure that the child's anxiety levels remain bearable.

3. **Shaping**. Here the child's speech patterns are developed. The child may begin without social communication, then gradually build a relationship with the therapist in which he feels sufficiently at ease to communicate nonverbally, after which he works toward eliciting sounds, consonants, words, sentences and ultimately spontaneous speech.

Stages of Therapy

Below are the four main stages of therapy: home sessions, school-based with the therapist, school-based with the therapist and peers and/or staff, and out of the school therapy room and into the classroom. These four main stages will be followed by the smaller steps of the sub-stages, with suggested activities within each stage.

Progression from one stage to the next depends on the pace at which the child has attained previous goals and an estimation of the boundaries of the child's comfort levels. **The sessions outlined below are just examples of how therapy could proceed. They should be modified according to the child's level and type of SM, his progress, and the therapist's intuition.** They may proceed faster with several sessions rolled into one, or may require smaller steps and more sessions. Remember to **always begin sessions with activities that the child has successfully accomplished previously** before attempting a new goal. There is huge room for the **therapist's creativity** in finding activities that appeal to the child, lower his anxiety, and are conducive to a warm therapist-child relationship.

Prior to beginning therapy, the child should be assessed, his speech patterns and baseline estimated, and parent and teacher interviews conducted, along with consideration of the predisposing and maintaining factors outlined above.

As well as facilitating a verbal, communicative relationship between the therapist and child, home sessions offer an opportunity to develop a supportive, productive relationship with the parents. At this time, initial guidance sessions may be held with the parents, helping them to nurture independence and social confidence in their children.

At the beginning of the therapy, several tasks should be given to the parents that will be helpful later on. In order to maximize the effectiveness of therapy, parents should be active partners with their own tasks to fulfill, as is described in full in the Parents' Manual.

Firstly, **parents should take it upon themselves to invite the child's classmates to their home as frequently as possible**. They are responsible for ensuring that a good time will be had by all during these visits, perhaps preparing enjoyable activities or games for these play-dates, and ensuring that bothersome elements, such as bossy older siblings (if an issue), are minimized. If the child speaks to the friend in these visits, the course of therapy will be greatly eased.

Secondly, the therapist, parents and teachers should, when possible, plan **parent visits to the school at least once a week** during which they work according to a scale of graded settings in which the child will speak to his parent/family member. For example, on the parent's first visit to the school, she may sit with her child in a secluded area of the yard and elicit speech from him. The following week she may sit in a less secluded part of the yard and the next week in a room within the school building. Similarly, the parent may initially sit with the child alone, and then gradually invite friends to join in the sessions. In this way, there is a parallel, parent-induced process of desensitization occurring together with the therapist's intervention. This is more fully described in the Parents' Manual (pages 21-22).

Stage 1: Home Sessions

Whenever possible, first sessions are conducted in the child's home or wherever the child speaks most comfortably. These must be planned in advance with the parent or sibling who will be present at the initial sessions. The idea is that the therapist will slip inconspicuously into the home setting, enabling the child to continue talking in her presence. Once the child speaks openly with the therapist at home, the sessions can be moved to the school or kindergarten.

Even before therapy begins, it is advisable for the family of the child to play with taping or filming devices in which the child and other family members record themselves for fun so that the child grows accustomed to being taped or filmed; this will be used later to facilitate therapy.

As mentioned before, it is important that the child is reasonably comfortable with the aim of each therapy session, and whenever possible, the sessions should be fun. This serves two purposes: When a child enjoys an activity, it distracts him from the intensity and stress of his endeavor to attain speech goals, and paradoxically makes them easier to attain. It also does wonders for motivation, engaging the child in the process of conquering selective mutism.

Here follow **concrete examples of how the stages may look**, following the principles outlined above. These descriptions are provided in order to give the therapist a picture of how to proceed with therapy. Clearly, **each child has his own baseline of speech in diverse settings, and will react in his unique way and pace to therapy; the stages and activities will have to be amended accordingly.** The therapist must use his understanding, judgment, and intuition to modify the sessions to fit the child.

Session 1-i
Location: Home
Aim: The child should speak naturally in the presence of the therapist.
In the initial session in the child's home, the therapist directs small talk to the parent or sibling, does not address the child directly, and makes herself so unobtrusive as to almost blend in with the furniture! In planning the meeting, the parent and the therapist must think of a way to ensure that the child is in the room with the therapist and the parent. This can be done by planning an activity that will be enjoyable and will keep the child in the room, yet won't be bombastic or something that the child has never done before—which could raise the child's suspicions and anxiety that something is aplot!

Activities: The parents should decide on activities according to the child's preferences —they should be enjoyable and engaging, and may include baking cookies, card games, board games, building activities, arts and crafts, etc. A family member leads the activity; the therapist is a fly-on-the-wall.

Session 1-ii
Location: Home
Aim: The child should play a game with family member(s) and therapist without the therapist directing speech to the child.
The parent plays a game or involves the child in an activity, and initially the therapist observes. In the second half hour, the therapist joins in the game, but does not direct speech to the child.

Activities: May include board games, memory games, lotto, puzzles, construction games, arts and crafts, sports, cooking, etc.

Session 1-iii
Location: Home
Aim: The child will play a game with family member(s) and therapist, including direct speech between therapist and child. The child will be taped or filmed for fun by a parent during the session and will play the tape back to family members.
Initially a game is played with family members and the therapist without direct speech between the child and the therapist, after which the therapist and family members play a game that includes direct speech between therapist and child.

Activities: As in session 1-ii.

Session 1-iv
Location: Home
Aim: The child will play a game just with the therapist, including direct speech between therapist and child. The child will be taped or filmed for fun during the session and will play the tape back to family members.
The therapist and child play games with direct speech between them. The child is taped by the family and plays back the tape to the family members in the presence of the therapist.

Activities: In the final home-based session, it is useful to play games or engage in activities that can be repeated during the following school-based session, such as board games, cards, and arts and crafts. The game hot/cold can be played—it is a good way to start the following school-based sessions and should be introduced at the home. The child hides a candy, and the therapist searches for it as the child says hot or cold depending on the proximity of the therapist to the treat. Then roles are reversed.

If, by the end of this session, the therapist and parents feel that the child is at ease talking and playing with the therapist, then the following sessions can take place at school. Sometimes, further home sessions are required before the child reaches a satisfactory level of comfort to enable changing locations.

Finalizing the home-based sessions
At the end of the home-based therapy sessions, the therapist should explain to the child that from now on the sessions will take place in school. The therapist should explain this in a light, natural way by saying that she works in the child's school, takes out children for enjoyable activities, and will take him out for sessions in school from now on, sometimes alone and sometimes with friends. She should explain that usually children really enjoy the sessions, as they involve games, arts and crafts, etc.

There may be cases in which it is not possible to carry out home sessions. For example, parents may be resistant or there may be children who do not speak at home. In these cases, therapy begins in the school or clinic and starts from the point of non-speech with the therapist (see Appendix 3: Guidelines for the Treatment of Selective Mutism without Home Sessions, page 125).

Whenever possible, it is highly preferable to hold initial home-based sessions before tackling the selective mutism in school; it shortens the length of therapy, involves parents and families in treatment, and enables the therapist to understand the child's optimum functioning.

Stage 2: School-Based with Therapist

The transition of therapy from home to school is delicate and requires sensitivity and understanding on the part of the therapist so that it may be carried out while maintaining the level of speech that had been reached between the therapist and child during the home sessions.

When speech that has been elicited at home with the therapist can be successfully transferred to the school, it greatly speeds up the process of establishing normal speech at school. Remember that **the sessions outlined below give a general idea of how therapy might proceed; in reality they will need to be tailored to the needs and pace of each and every child.**

Before moving the therapy to the school setting, the therapist must update the teacher regarding progress and arrange with her a suitable time and place for therapy to continue. The therapist should have a private room in the school that will be available for the therapy sessions and ensure that it is stocked with the required materials— arts and crafts supplies, games, and recording equipment. The teacher should be advised on how to explain the sessions to the rest of the class. Normalization is the guiding principle. Therapy should not put the child with SM in the limelight in the eyes of his peers. A sample explanation by the teacher could be the following: "Sara sometimes takes children to her room for various activities. She will be taking Johnny for the next few weeks."

The start of school-based therapy sessions is a time to consider what the teacher can do to hasten the child's improvement. Simultaneous with the parents' and therapist's interventions, there should be **a parallel and interconnected teacher's intervention.** The teacher should consider four main goals: establishing a communicative relationship with the child, helping the child to take gradual, controlled steps toward speech, lowering the child's anxiety, and building his self-confidence in school. This is fully described in the Teacher's Manual. The therapist should read the Teacher's Manual and sit with the teacher to consider how to implement the described interventions.

For example, the parents could tape the child every day at home, so that the teacher would listen to the tape in the child's presence every morning in school, at a fixed time in a private setting. In this way, the teacher will be hearing indirect speech from the child every day, and the barrier keeping the teacher from hearing his voice will come crashing down! For a fuller description see the Teacher's Manual, pages 52-57.

Session 2-i
Location: School therapy room
Aim: The child should speak with the therapist in a therapy room within the school. Please note that this is described here as one session, but may require several in order for the child to speak freely to the therapist in school.

The therapist takes the child to the therapy room inside the school. Whenever possible, she should have a tape of the child speaking at home that was recorded by the parents during the previous home-based sessions. This can be played as soon as the child comes into the room and initiates the session by breaking one barrier—his voice is present in school, on the tape.

Games can be played which require minimal or rote speech. A good way to proceed is to play hot/cold—which has previously been played at home—in which the child must say "hot" or "cold," guiding the therapist towards a hidden treat, and may simultaneously bang a tambourine louder or softer.

Other examples of games requiring a defined amount of speech are happy families or throwing a ball to one another saying your name (or other category such as clothes, foods, colors, etc.) each time you throw it. If the child speaks to the therapist, further games previously enjoyed at home can be played. If the child fails to talk, games should be played that require nonverbal communication and noise production, including playing musical instruments and banging.

A note about whispering:
Sometimes when a child with SM begins to speak in school, he whispers. The therapist should not accept this, but should consider how to help the child achieve audible speech, as whispering can itself become an entrenched and nonfunctional way of communicating. The therapist

should work toward raising the volume of the child's speech using behavioral shaping methods. The parents can be helpful here again. For example, if the child is talking to the therapist in school in a whisper, a parent may be invited to join in a session at the school with the therapist and child. The **parent-child session** would take place in the school therapy room, initially without the therapist. The parent begins the session playing with the child games that require speech, such as hot/cold, blind man's buff, card games, recording activities, and ball games that require speech (for example, each time a ball is thrown the thrower has to say the name of the person to whom he is throwing it). The parent does not accept whispering, and once the child is speaking at a normal volume, the therapist comes into the room but does not join in the game. Gradually, the therapist approaches the child and his parent and eventually joins in the game. This may occur in one session, or may require several parent-child-therapist school-based sessions.

Sometimes the child stalls at the whispering stage, and activities in which the **child's whisper is amplified** may be needed. This could include games in which the child speaks into a microphone or makes the volume display on a tape recorder show increased volume. Use of a Madonna microphone which the child wears is often fun for the child and allows him to be mobile during games. For example, the child may already be whispering answers and plays hangman with the therapist, during which he whispers each letter he guesses into a microphone so that it can be heard out loud. Similarly, this could take place within a game of twenty questions or I spy with the child answering into a microphone. Again, this could occur in one session, or it may take several sessions of structured steps. If this does not spontaneously engender speech, a graduated series of steps can be planned in which the child speaks into a microphone when the therapist is outside the room, then he speaks into a microphone when the therapist is inside the room looking away from him, and finally she looks at the child when he talks. Then the volume is lowered on the amplifier so that the child must speak louder to be heard, and finally the volume is switched off, leaving the child speaking aloud without amplification.

If the child succeeds in talking to the therapist in the initial sessions, then the therapist can jump to session 2-vii, page 104. If the child does not speak to the therapist in the initial school-based sessions, continue with sessions 2-ii to 2-vi below.

Sometimes the child fails to speak to the therapist in these first sessions, in which case a structured behavior modification program can be utilized with the help of the parents. An example of this is outlined below in sessions 2-ii to 2-vi. It should be adapted to the needs and pace of each individual child.

Session 2-ii
Location: School therapy room
Aim: The child should speak to a parent/family member in the presence of the therapist in school.
The therapist arranges for a parent or family member with whom the child speaks to meet the child in the therapy room. The parent and child remain alone in the room for half an hour after which the therapist enters. During the time in which the parent and child are alone, they should engage in activities described above—playing a recording of the child or playing hot/cold, board games, or arts and crafts that the child likes and that require a minimal amount of speech. When the therapist enters, she remains in the room but does not participate in the activities or comment; she simply listens to the child speaking with his parent. This may occur in one session or may take several sessions.

Session 2-iii
Location: School therapy room
Aim: The child should speak to a parent/family member and the therapist in school.
The family member comes again to the school therapy room, engages the child in activities requiring speech, and after a few minutes, the therapist enters the room. If the child seems ready, the therapist joins in the activities and speaks to the child. If the child speaks directly with

the therapist, continue with session 2-vi. If the child is reticent to speak to the therapist, further sessions are required. If after further sessions it seems that a more structured approach is required, stimulus fading can be tried as described below.

Session 2-iv
Location: School therapy room
Aim: The child should speak to a parent/family member and the therapist in school using stimulus shaping ("sliding in").

This is a version of stimulus shaping developed by Johnson and Wintgens (2001). Here the parent engages her child in an activity in which rote speech is required, and the therapist gradually comes within hearing distance and eventually joins in so that the child speaks to her. For example, the parent and child could throw a ball to each other, and each time they throw it they have to say a number in turn. They begin the game alone in the room. After a while, the door is opened and the therapist, who is sitting outside the room, hears the child's voice. After this, the therapist enters the room and sits with her back to the child. Finally, the therapist will sit facing the child and will then join in the game. This may be done in one session or may need to be broken down into several sessions. The sliding in procedure should be explained to the child before carrying it out, in a way in which the child will feel the least anxiety possible. The therapist may include a small treat in the center of the circle of people engaged in "sliding in", and the child could receive a candy after each round of the game. The remainder of the time in each session once the sliding in is finished, if the child is not ready for further verbal communication, can be taken up with games played by the therapist, parent, and child that require nonverbal communication, listening to tapes of the child previously recorded at home, and playing games that generate noise, such as musical instruments.

Session 2-v
Location: School therapy room
Aim: The child should speak to a parent/family member and the therapist in school.
Once "sliding in" is successfully carried out, the parent should continue to come to sessions until the child is speaking comfortably to the therapist; activities should be undertaken that employ rote language and gradually more spontaneous language can be encouraged. This may occur in one session or may require several meetings. The therapist and parent must use their understanding and intuition to decide at which point the parent need not come to sessions.

Activities: May include hot/cold, ball games, card games such as happy families, commercial and board games (such as Bingo, Lotto, Guess Who, Submarines, Taboo), arts and crafts, etc.

Session 2-vi
Location: School therapy room
Aim: The child should speak to the therapist in school without the family member.
Once the child feels comfortable speaking to the therapist in school in the presence of the family member, sessions should continue without the family member present. The therapist should play games and engage in activities that the child has enjoyed in previous sessions to give a feeling of continuity. The sessions can be structured so that they start with games employing one-word answers, gradually progressing to activities that require more language and, eventually, spontaneous speech. Ample use should be made of playing prerecorded songs, stories, or speech of the child.

Activities: Could include hot/cold, Chinese whispers, word guessing games such as I spy, twenty questions and hangman, card games such as happy families, commercial and board games such as Bingo, Lotto and Submarines, activities employing a combination of physical activity and speech such as ball games and blind man's buff, arts and crafts, etc.

Session 2-vii
Location: School therapy room
Aim: Consolidation of the child's speech with the therapist in school without the family member.

In the previous session the child managed to talk to the therapist in the school therapy room without the parent/family member present. This should be consolidated before peers are included in the sessions. The therapist must use her intuition to decide how many such sessions are required. In these meetings, the therapist follows the format of previous sessions, partaking in activities that require the child to speak and varying these activities to include games that the child did not play previously with his parents. Once the child is comfortable speaking to the therapist, he is ready to progress to Stage 3.

Activities: Could include hot/cold, Chinese whispers, ball games, guessing games such as I spy, twenty questions and hangman, word games like child and therapist making up a story taking turns adding one word at a time, and "I went to the store and bought..." with therapist and child adding bought items in turn and recalling previously mentioned items, card games such as happy families, commercial and board games such as Bingo, Lotto, Submarines, Guess Who and Taboo, arts and crafts, etc.

Stage 3: School-Based with Therapist and Friends/Teachers

Once the child is comfortable speaking to the therapist alone in the therapy room in school or kindergarten, the next variable to change is the people present in the room, usually starting by including peers in the sessions. At the beginning of therapy, the parents were encouraged to invite the child's friends to their home and to ensure that pleasant activities took place during these play-dates. Now with input from the teacher, the parents, and the child, the therapist determines who are the child's best friends and with which friends he speaks at home and at school. If he speaks with certain classmates at home or in school, these should be the first ones to join in the therapy sessions. Permission must be requested from the parents of the children to be added to the sessions, as well as from the teacher.

A similar process occurs in this stage to that outlined in Stages 1 and 2. The therapist invites children to join the sessions, changing one variable at a time so that the games are similar, but an extra person is added. Once the child speaks with the therapist and one child, another child is added. To illustrate this process, here follow postulated Stage 3 sessions.

Session 3-i
Location: School therapy room
Aim: Child should speak to therapist and classmate in therapy room.
A classmate is invited to join in the session. It is preferable that this is a child with whom the child speaks at home and whose company the child enjoys. The plan in this session is to go from taped speech, to whispered speech, to rote speech, to spontaneous speech. Here again, the child may pass through all these stages in one session, or several sessions may be required.

Activities: It is advisable that the session begins with playing a tape or showing a film of the child that has been used in previous sessions. In this way, his voice will immediately be present in the room. The next activity could be Chinese whispers, where the child with SM is always the middle child so that he only has to whisper and not say the word out loud. The next activity could be a game employing rote speech out loud, such as throwing a ball and saying your name as you throw it. The following activity could be playing happy families where a certain card must be asked for.

Some children will not progress through more than one of these stages in the first session, and others will go through to spontaneous speech with the classmate in one session. If the child stalls at one of these activities, it is a sign that he may require a few sessions to get through all the stages. In this case, the pace must be slowed so that the child may have one session in which a tape of his voice is heard and simultaneously engage in games in which nonverbal communication is called for. In the following session the tape could be heard again, and Chinese whispers would be played. In this way, in each session a new variable would be introduced.

If a child fails to progress through a given stage as expected, the therapist must return to the previous stage and reincorporate whichever elements she thinks would stimulate progress. For example, if a child fails to talk with a friend, one of several courses of action could be required: It could be that he needs more sessions to consolidate his speech with the therapist; perhaps a parent should come in for one or two sessions with the child and his friend; maybe what is needed is that the therapist should conduct a couple of home-based sessions with the child with SM together with his friend, after which she would meet with the child and his friend in the school therapy room.

Session 3-ii
Location: School therapy room
Aim: Consolidation of child speaking to therapist and classmate in school therapy room.
The child plays games requiring speech with his classmate and the therapist, starting, as always, with games successfully played in the previous sessions and adding further activities and games. Thus his speech in this setting will be consolidated.

Activities: Could include hot/cold, Chinese whispers, throwing a ball and saying a name or object within a category, happy families, lotto, commercial board games such as Guess Who and Taboo, taping the children and playing it back to them, puppet shows, charades, word games previously described, I spy, twenty questions, hangman, arts and crafts etc.

Session 3-iii
Location: School therapy room
Aim: Child should speak to the therapist and two classmates in school therapy room.
Here an additional classmate joins the session. This should preferably be a classmate liked by the child and one with whom he has spoken outside school. The process is parallel to that in session 3-i, beginning with taped speech from previous sessions or from home, followed by games requiring individual words or rote speech, and then activities requiring more spontaneous speech. As above, the child may progress through all these stages in one session, or it may take several sessions.

Activities: As above in 3-i and 3-ii.

Session 3-iv
Location: School therapy room
Aim: Consolidation of child speaking to therapist and two classmates in school therapy room.
The child should play games requiring speech with his classmates and the therapist, starting, as always, with games successfully played in the previous session, and adding further activities and games.

Activities: Could include hot/cold, Chinese whispers, ball games, word-guessing games such as twenty questions, hangman and I spy, word games such as the children and therapist making up a story taking turns adding one word at a time, and "I went to the store and bought…" with therapist and children adding bought items in turn and recalling previously mentioned items, card games such as happy families, commercial and board games such as Bingo, Lotto, Submarines, Guess Who and Taboo, blind man's buff, arts and crafts, etc.

Session 3-v
Location: School therapy room
Aim: The child should speak in the school therapy room with three classmates or a varied configuration of classmates.

The idea for the remainder of the sessions in this stage is to either add further children or to vary the configuration of children in the sessions, so that each session includes one or more children with whom the child with SM has spoken and a new classmate with whom the child has not yet spoken in school. The activities are similar to those in the other Stage 3 sessions, and the rules are the same: to change one variable at a time, and if the child stalls, either to go back to the last stage in which he successfully achieved the goal and consolidate it before going further, or to make the steps taken toward new goals smaller and more gradual.

One method to increase generalization in order to include peers and even staff in one fell swoop is to **prepare a puppet show or a play with a group of children** in the therapy room and then to **film it and play it to other children and/or staff**. Alternatively, one could invite a group of children and teachers to come into the therapy room and see the performance once it has been prepared. This depends on the child's response to the idea of performing; sometimes in the guise of a character in a play or puppet show, speech is possible in front of people with whom the child has not previously spoken. A cardinal rule here is to be open with the child when suggesting the show and not to go forward if it seems to be too anxiety provoking.

It is possible at this stage to invite staff with whom the child does not speak into the therapy room, much as has been done with classmates. This is done by inviting a teacher either by herself, or together with a couple of children with whom the child already speaks in the therapy room and playing tapes and games in a way similar to how classmates were included in session 3-i (page 105). Here the therapist must judge which will be the child's path of least resistance, either generalizing the child's speech by taking the group outside the therapy room or including adults within the therapy room. The choice should be made according to what the therapist feels will cause the child less anxiety, and her estimation of what is likely to be more natural and effective.

Once the child speaks comfortably in the school therapy room with the therapist and several children and/or teachers it is time to generalize the speech to the wider context of the school beyond the four walls of the therapy room.

Stage 4: Taking the Therapy out of the Therapy Room and into the Classroom

Now that the child speaks freely in the therapy room, the aim is to enable him to speak in the larger school environment. The same behavioral techniques previously employed in stages 1 to 3 are used here. At this stage, the sessions initially take place in a public space in the school such as a corridor or yard and ultimately are held in the classroom. It is frequently the case that as there is improvement in the therapy room, parallel processes will occur in other contexts, and the child will begin to speak in the classroom or yard. Usually, however, some structured help is required to shape speech so that it fully generalizes to the classroom.

Session 4-i
Location: School—public space (corridor, hallway, yard, etc.)
Aim: The child should speak in a school common space with the therapist, or with the therapist plus one classmate.
As in all the above steps, one variable is changed at a time, in this case the setting. The therapist will have to judge whether it will be easier for the child to speak in this new setting with her alone, or with

the therapist plus one peer with whom he has spoken in previous sessions in the therapy room.

The context should be a public space in the school that is sheltered—not too much through traffic—where the little group can sit at a table and play games. The activities should be those successfully performed in the previous stages, again ordered according to verbal output, from recorded speech, to one word or rote responses through to spontaneous speech.

For the sake of clarity, this is presented as one session, but in reality, it may need several sessions in order for the child to reach spontaneous speech in this public setting.

Sometimes it is easier for the child to begin in an outdoor setting such as the schoolyard, and once the child is comfortable speaking outdoors, the little group may be moved to an indoor common space.

Activities: Could include hot/cold, Chinese whispers, guessing games such as I spy, twenty questions, and hangman, word games with physical activity like throwing a ball and saying a name within a category, recording one another and listening to the recordings, playing with mobile phones (for example members of the group phoning one another from varying distances and locations within the school), happy families, board games such as Taboo, Guess Who and Lotto, arts and crafts etc.

Session 4-ii
Location: School—public space (corridor, hallway, yard, etc.)
Aim: The child should speak in the school common space with the therapist and several classmates.
Once the child speaks in the common space with the therapist and one child, several children can be added, starting with those with whom the child has previously spoken. The same caution should be taken to ensure that there is a gradual increase in the speech

requirements of the activities employed, moving from low speech output to spontaneous speech.

Activities are as above in 4-i.

Session 4-iii
Location: School—classroom (in a relatively sheltered corner of the room)
Aim: The child should speak in the classroom with the therapist.
The therapist and child sit in a corner of the classroom; the child should have his back to the rest of the class. The activities again should be those previously enjoyed, and requiring gradually increasing amounts of speech output—beginning with a game that requires little speech, such as happy families or arts and crafts, and moving on to games which may require more speech or, alternatively, gradually incorporating conversations between the therapist and child.

Frequently the child will speak quietly or in a whisper, and it may take a few sessions to shape his speech so that it is audible to other people present in the classroom. It may be preferable to hold the first kindergarten or classroom session during recess when the classroom is empty, followed by sessions during periods where the rest of the children are in the room.

Activities: May include Chinese whispers, guessing games such as I spy, hangman and twenty questions, word games including child and therapist making up a story taking turns adding one word at a time, "I went to the store and bought…" with therapist and child adding bought items in turn and recalling previously mentioned items, card games such as happy families, commercial and board games such as Bingo, Lotto, Submarines, Guess Who and Taboo, games requiring physical activity together with speech such as ball games played while sitting down opposite one another, arts and crafts etc.

Session 4-iv
Location: School—classroom (in a relatively sheltered corner of the room)
Aim: The child should speak in the classroom with the therapist and a classmate.
This is as above in session 4-iii but includes a classmate with whom the child has spoken in previous sessions in the activities. If it is felt that consolidation is required, several such sessions can be held, including more children, and varying the children participating in the sessions.

Activities: As in session 4-iii

Session 4-v
Location: School—classroom (in a relatively sheltered corner of the room)
Aim: The child should speak in the classroom with the therapist and the classmate.
This is as above in session 4-iii, but now the child faces the classroom from the corner where previously he had his back to the other children.

Activities: As above.

Session 4-vi
Location: School—classroom (in a relatively sheltered corner of the room)
Aim: The child should speak in the classroom with the therapist, classmate and teacher.
Here the teacher is included in the little group in the classroom corner. As before, small steps are taken within this stage. First the teacher is passive but close to the group as they are playing a game in which rote speech is required. Then she is passive and next to the group. Then she joins in the game without speaking directly to the child, and finally she engages in direct speech with the child. Again, this may occur in one session or in several. If the child finds it hard to speak to the teacher or in her presence, preparing and performing a puppet show or play for the class could help, as described in session 3-v, page 108.

Activities: As above in session 4-iii.

Session 4-vii
Location: School—classroom, at the child's desk
Aim: The child should speak in the classroom at his desk with the therapist.
Here the aim is to generalize the child's speech further so that he speaks sitting at his place in class, or at a group table in kindergarten. The therapist sits with the child at his desk during a regular lesson and elicits speech from him in a gentle and non-threatening way. It is important not to be satisfied with a whisper, but to elicit audible speech.

Activities: The child participates in whatever the class is doing.

Session 4-viii
Location: School—classroom, at the child's desk
Aim: The child should speak in the classroom at his desk with the teacher, while the therapist is by his side.
The therapist sits next to the child at his desk during a regular lesson and the therapist elicits speech from him. Then the teacher asks him an easy question close up, which the child answers. If the child seems ready, the teacher can then ask a question (which is easy, requires a one-word answer, and whose answer is certainly known by the child) in front of the rest of the class.

Activities: Whatever the class is doing.

Session 4-ix
Location: School—classroom, at the child's desk
Aim: The child should speak in the classroom at his desk with the teacher when the therapist is not by his side.
The therapist sits next to the child at his desk during a regular lesson and the therapist elicits speech from him. Then the teacher asks him an easy question close up which the child answers. After this, the therapist moves away from the child, and the teacher asks him another

easy question from close up. Finally the therapist goes out of the room, but remains by the door, visible from within the class, and the teacher again approaches the child and asks him a question requiring a verbal response.

Activities: Whatever the class is doing.

Further sessions consolidating the child's speech in the classroom or kindergarten will most likely be required, enabling the child to continue speaking without the presence of the therapist.

At this point it is hoped that the child is responding verbally to questions from his teacher and interacting verbally with his peers. It is possible that pockets of selective mutism remain within the school—perhaps difficulty talking to other staff members, older children, etc. Similar methods can be employed to tackle these last bastions of non-speech, and **it is important not to end therapy prematurely**. When it is not viable to continue therapy, and the child now speaks with his teacher, it is often possible to guide the teacher so that she can ensure that the speech generalizes further until the child can respond verbally to any person who addresses him in private. Similarly, there may be some situations outside the school in which the child still fails to speak, such as to certain family members, in stores, etc. Here the parent may be guided as to how to further develop the child's speech and social communication. This is described more fully in the Parents' Manual.

It is clear that for some shy children, many social tasks may remain daunting, such as speaking in front of a class, going to friends' homes for the first time, and so on. In much the same way as described above, stepwise behavioral interventions can be useful and may be implemented by the teacher, parents, or therapist. For example, if a child finds it hard to speak in front of the class, he may be encouraged to speak about something he knows well in front of a small group and be praised for so doing. Similarly, a child for whom going to a friend's house for the first time may be daunting might be helped by a gradual program implemented by his parents. For example, first the friend comes to his house, then he goes to the friend's house with his parent. After that, the parent accompanies him but stays for a brief time, and finally the child stays alone at the friend's house. Small but sure steps that allow gradual exposure are best.

Once the therapist terminates therapy, a case manager in the school should be appointed—this could be the teacher, assistant, or school psychologist—who will consider the child's ongoing functioning in school and implement interventions when needed. The school case manager may have to ensure that new staff members are aware of the child's sensitivity, or consider in advance possible pitfalls intrinsic to transitions, so that steps can be taken to safeguard continued improvement in the child's social communication skills.

Sometimes, once normative speech is acquired, other difficulties become apparent that require treatment. These could include speech impediments requiring speech therapy, shyness in social situations causing discomfort or other emotional issues that call for continued therapy. Now that the child speaks, these issues can be addressed and hopefully eased, with the now verbal child participating in the required treatment.

Usually the acquisition of normative speech exerts a powerful effect over related areas in the child's psychological makeup and social development; he is now able to benefit from the wealth of social situations open to him where previously he was withdrawn. He may now see himself as a normal child who speaks when spoken to and who does not have to exert constant control not to talk. His anxiety level drops, and his self-confidence soars.

Appendix 1

Speaking Checklist:
Where and to Whom the Child Speaks

Key: F=freely, M=minimally, W=whispering

Location: To Whom:	Home	Park	School yard	School class-room	School inside public areas	Friend's or relative's house	Unfamiliar place	Store
Mother								
Father								
Brothers								
Sisters								
Grandmother								
Grandfather								
Uncles								
Aunts								
Cousins								

Child's teacher											
Other teachers											
Teaching assistant											
Family friends: adults											
Family friends: children											
Neighbors: adults											
Neighbors: children											
School friends											
Strangers: children											
Strangers: adults											
Store assistants											
Doctor											

Appendix 2

Cognitive-Behavioral Techniques for Older Children and Teenagers

The treatment of choice for young children with selective mutism (SM) is usually behavioral with certain cognitive components. This is the treatment plan outlined in the manuals. Behavioral treatments attempt to alter the child's behavior in small structured steps. In the case of SM, the aim is to guide the child from silence to speech in all settings. With young children, certain cognitive elements may be incorporated in the treatment, including an explanation about selective mutism, how many other children suffer from it, and how it generally responds well to treatment (psycho-education, normalization, and belief in the child's ability to change his behavior). The course of therapy is set by the therapist, parents, and teachers according to their understanding of the needs, anxiety level, and strengths of the child.

With older children, and certainly with teenagers, the cognitive elements of therapy become more prominent. As the child matures and becomes more introspective, the therapy has to be run along more egalitarian lines in which the child becomes an active partner working with the therapist to understand his condition. Together with the therapist, he will consider and select steps that can be taken to enable speech, will share the responsibility of achieving these goals, and will assess his behavior retrospectively. In addition, there must be fuller disclosure by the therapist to the child regarding her insights and treatment plan.

Thus the therapeutic balance between the behavioral steps and the cognitive elements changes with older children, as greater weight is given to their understanding and ability to implement behavioral steps based on this insight. The pros and cons of adding cognitive components must be carefully weighed by the therapist, as often a heavily skewed behavioral approach works best even for older children. The child's nature, level of introspection, anxiety, and response to each stage of treatment must be considered in order to ascertain how much of a cognitive approach will be productive.

Here follows a summary of cognitive components that can be incorporated into treatment, in addition to behavioral steps such as those described in the manual. For a more thorough description of CBT programs for children, which may be adapted to and integrated with the behavioral SM treatment described in this manual, see References section (page 131) for child CBT programs.

Cognitive Elements within Cognitive-Behavioral Therapy

The methods described below redress the balance between the cognitive and behavioral components of therapy with older children. It should be borne in mind that **the backbone of CBT therapy for people with SM of all ages remains behavioral.** Thus it is based on the behavioral building blocks of therapy described in the manuals. This translation of insight into actions must always occur in order to conquer SM.

Assessment:
Before embarking on therapy, the therapist, parents, and teacher conduct a thorough assessment of the child's speaking patterns, developmental etiology, social skills and activity, family traits, etc. as proposed in the manual. After the initial home-based sessions are held, as outlined in the manual, during which the child speaks to the therapist, sessions could be held with the child in order to understand how he perceives the SM and to learn about his personality, his strengths, his weaknesses, and how he experiences his life. Even with older children and teens, the therapist must exert utmost caution so

as not to exceed the young person's level of tolerable anxiety in these assessment sessions.

Psycho-education:
A stage of **psycho-education** may then take place in which the child receives an explanation about SM: how it affects children, how it responds to treatment, and how it is usually anxiety-based. Important elements here are **normalization**—showing the child how many others are in the same boat, the **adaptive value of anxiety**—it protects you from danger, and an understanding of **how anxiety affects the body**—increased heartbeat, readiness to react etc. The therapist's belief in the child's strengths and in his ability to progress should be manifest.

Relaxation techniques:
Once the young person understands how anxiety affects his body and mind, he may learn techniques that will ease his anxiety. This includes deep breathing techniques, flexing and releasing muscles, and guided imagery. It should be noted that many teenagers are resistant to learning relaxation techniques and if this is the case, there is no point in pursuing these methods.

Understanding the event-thoughts-feelings-behavior connection:
The young person may learn how his thoughts regarding any event affect his feelings and behavior. There are several possible ways of thinking about any given situation. He may learn how to channel his thoughts so that they will be more adaptive, optimistic, and confident, less scared and defeatist. This will affect his feelings and ultimately his behavior. He may learn how to analyze different situations to see how his thoughts may have been maladaptive and consider more positive ways of thinking. When young people learn how to channel their thoughts, it gives them an increased sense of control over how they perceive and experience their lives. The young person may apply this

newfound skill to how he feels in situations in which he is required to speak or engage in other daunting social communication behavior.

Building a stepladder of goals:
Throughout this process the aim, together with increased self-awareness, is facilitating speech and improved social functioning. Based on the child's and the therapist's understanding of the relative difficulty he experiences speaking in different settings, they build together a stepladder of goals which will take the young person from nonverbal communication to speech with different people and in various settings. Table 3 on the following page shows an example of a stepladder built for a child in the school-sessions stage of therapy, which would take place after the home-sessions stage. Ben is already talking freely to the therapist in school and the aim in this stepladder it to enable him to talk to a friend (in this case, Dan) in school.

Table 3: Example of a stepladder of goals for a child in stage 3: School-based with therapist, Ben, and another child.

Brave Ben's Goal Ladder

Ladder of tasks	Success -Date
Dan joins in sessions with Ruth (therapist) and me (Ben) in school. I will play a recording to him that I made at home of me talking to my brother. I will whisper to Ruth in the game of Chinese whispers with Ruth and Dan.	10.8.2011
Play Chinese whispers with Ruth and Dan, I will whisper to Dan.	
Play hangman with Ruth and Dan, I will whisper the letters to Dan.	
Play hangman with Ruth and Dan, I will whisper the letters to Dan from the other side of the room.	
Play 20 questions with Dan and Ruth, at the end of the game Dan will go out of the room, he will stand next to the <u>closed door</u>, and I will reveal the answer to Dan in a regular voice.	
Play 20 questions with Dan and Ruth, at the end of the game Dan will go out of the room, he will stand next to the <u>open door</u>, and I will reveal the answer to Dan in a regular voice.	
Play 20 questions with Dan and Ruth, at the end of the game Dan stays <u>in the room</u>, he will cover his eyes, and I will reveal the answer to him in a regular voice.	
Play 20 questions with Dan and Ruth, at the end of the game Dan stays in the room and I will reveal the answer to him in a regular voice.	

Play snap with Dan, when we get the same card I will say "snap".	
Play with Dan and Ruth "I went to the store and bought..." adding bought items in turn and recalling previously mentioned items.	

In the sessions corresponding to the goals in the stepladder, each session will begin by playing games that the child has previously successfully managed, so that all the sessions would begin with playing a recording of Ben made at home, and a game of Chinese whispers, in which first Ben would whisper to Ruth, then to Dan. Once the goal has been reached in each session, further games could be played involving arts and crafts, or games that Ben enjoys, which employ communication that Ben is able to use at that point. Once Ben successfully completes the above stepladder of goals, a new one would be built which would help him perhaps to talk to additional children, or to speak to Dan in a more open setting.

Desensitization techniques:
The child is helped by the therapist to approach and achieve the goals set in the stepladder by using some or all of the techniques mentioned here, including relaxation techniques, guided imagery, positive thinking, etc., in order to speak in more settings and to a greater number of people. Stimulus shaping, "sliding in," and stimulus fading can be used, which are described in the Therapist's Manual.

Assessing success:
The young person and the therapist assess his performance in approaching and achieving each goal on the stepladder and fine-tune the upcoming tasks on the stepladder, taking into consideration his functioning on previous steps.

Rewards and self-rewards:
Rewards may be incorporated for attempting to reach or for reaching a goal. Young people may learn how to speak to themselves (self-talk)

in order to feel braver and more competent, which helps them move up the stepladder, and to praise themselves and feel good about their behavior.

Assertiveness and social skills training:
Especially with older children, failure to speak may have left its mark and developed into a more generalized social anxiety disorder. In such cases, together with the therapy aimed at facilitating speech, the above and further CBT techniques may be used to increase the young person's assertiveness and social skills.

Behavioral axes still prominent:
While the balance between the cognitive and the behavioral axes shifts as the child grows older, it is important to retain the goal of speech in all settings to all people. As a child grows towards adulthood, the lack of normal speech becomes increasingly anomalous and exceptional. A teenager who fails to speak sees himself as different and lacking in a basic social communication skill. As with younger children, the acquisition of normal speech outside the home is paramount and, once achieved, usually engenders a ripple effect: a burst of self-confidence, and feelings of competence.

Importance of working with parents and teachers:
As stressed in the manuals, the families and school staff should be active partners in the quest for normal speech and social communication. They should be consulted regarding all stages of the therapy, from assessment to the implementation of behavioral goals. Both the parents and teachers should have interventions that complement and supplement the therapist's treatment, as described in the manuals. In this way, the selective mutism will be combated on all fronts simultaneously with the aim of normalizing speech in all of the environments in which the young person lives.

Appendix 3

Guidelines for the Treatment of Selective Mutism without Home Sessions

While it is highly preferable to hold initial treatment sessions at the child's home, as this usually significantly shortens the length of the therapy, it is not always feasible. In such cases, sessions take place at school alone.

Whenever possible, effort should be made to maintain fluid and open contact and collaboration with parents as described in the manual, because even when treatment occurs exclusively at school, parents potentially remain an important contributing factor to successful treatment. They should be consulted in the assessment stage, given the Parents' Manual, and guided regarding their implementation of the parents' interventions as well as their management of their child's selective mutism. When parents are willing and able to assist in taping their child at home for use in the school sessions and can hold playing-talking sessions with their child in school or kindergarten as described in the manuals, this will greatly assist the course of therapy. So prior to beginning treatment with the child at school, meetings should be held with the parents in order to consult with them, guide them, and ensure that they will carry out their part in the treatment triangle of parents-school-therapist as much as possible.

Course of Treatment Beginning in School

When treatment begins at school, the beneficial jump-start of initial home sessions is lost. The aim of the home sessions is to enable the child to talk to the therapist with relative ease and speed by slotting in inconspicuously at home. When starting directly in school, speech has to be developed within the school setting, which is often a far more challenging task. All the principles regarding sessions, and the behavioral tools for shaping speech described in the manual are still relevant; however, the starting point of the school sessions will be the baseline of the child's speech in school, which is usually non-speech to adults.

The child will meet you for the first time in school, and the principle described in the Therapist's Manual regarding the playfulness and light character of therapy should be borne in mind when introducing yourself to the child. This helps to ensure the enjoyable, relaxed nature of the sessions, which in turn allows anxiety levels to remain low. The therapist can be introduced as someone who works in the school and takes children for play sessions, sometimes alone and sometimes with friends. The level and nature of further explanations—the cognitive component of therapy—depends on the age and developmental stage of the child and whether he initiates further discussion of the aims of the sessions, as outlined in the Therapist's Manual.

The therapy will proceed according to the stages outlined in the Therapist's Manual, but starting from stage 2-ii, page 101. In the original program, which begins with home-based sessions, this is the stage at which the child fails to speak to the therapist once the sessions are moved to the school.

If at all possible, **initial school-based sessions should be set up to resemble the home sessions as closely as possible**. If the parents are active partners in the therapy, they may be invited to the initial sessions so that the child will speak to them freely in the therapy room at school. The therapist will gradually and as inconspicuously as possible join in the sessions.

All sessions including a parent must be carefully planned with the parent beforehand, including which activities and games will be played in the session, how the parent will explain them to the child, and having a playful attitude to the sessions. All this is elaborated on in the Therapist's Manual.

In the first session, a parent (or sibling or other family member) may come to the therapy room and play with the child as previously planned with the therapist, without the therapist being present. The games and activities should be according to the preferences of the child so that it will be a pleasant experience. **The activities should require at least a minimal amount of speech,** or the parent can engage the child in conversation during the activity. For suggestions of activities, see the sessions' outlines in the Therapist's Manual, pages 101-104. Recordings of the child from home should be played during these sessions, such as the child interviewing siblings, singing, or reading. The parent-child sessions should take place uninterrupted in **a closed therapy room in the school** with only the parent present, enabling the child to speak freely with the parent. The parent should come several times until the child is speaking freely with the parent in the closed therapy room.

Once this is achieved, the **therapist will gradually insert herself in the proceedings,** as is described in sessions 2-ii to 2-vii (pages 101-104) in the Therapist's Manual. After that, therapy may continue as outlined in the Therapist's Manual.

Initial school-based sessions without familial presence:
If a family member cannot be present at the initial school-based sessions, then the therapist begins sessions in which she utilizes techniques to elicit speech in school without the parents' presence in the sessions. Whenever possible, it is important nevertheless to include the parents and family in the therapy in other ways, as described in the manual, including consulting them about preparing the treatment plan, working with them on possible anxiety issues of their own, and guiding them regarding the implementation of their interventions at home and in school.

If the child speaks to a classmate outside or inside school, it may be possible to include this friend in the sessions described above (with his parents' permission) and then to follow the steps from 2-ii on (page 101), as described in the Therapist's Manual, with the friend substituting for the family member. The sessions would need to be structured in a way in which the friend experiences the sessions as games and activities and, unlike the parents, is in no way involved in the planning or responsibility for the sessions.

All the therapy guidelines set out in the Therapist's Manual still hold true, including taking small, sure steps that are tolerable in terms of the child's anxiety level and ensuring that the sessions are pleasant and whenever possible fun for the child.

The therapist in school should plan a behavioral program in which the aim is to develop a relationship with the child that is initially nonverbal and that gradually progresses to eliciting sounds and eventually speech in the therapy room in school.

When the parents are unavailable to participate in the sessions, **then the initial school-based sessions** have the aim of establishing a relationship in which **the child feels at ease with the therapist.** Activities for these sessions should be according to the child's baseline of social communication and should have no speech requirements; non verbal communication requirements must be in the range of the child's current abilities within the therapist–child relationship. Activities could be telling or reading stories, arts and crafts, card or board games, etc.

Once the child is playing comfortably with the therapist, the steps are structured to include **nonverbal communication**, such as nodding, pointing, and gestures. When the child is ready, full-body gestures such as acting in games like charades can be included.

The following stage incorporates games that include **noise production**—for example, playing musical instruments, clapping, stamping, etc.

The next stage could be **eliciting sounds** coming from the mouth of the child within the framework of games as described in the manual, which may be clicking of the tongue or sounds such as "shhh" or "t." For example, a ball may be thrown between the therapist and the child, and each time it is thrown, the thrower makes the sound "shhh".

The hardest transition is usually between these nonverbal sounds and **speaking real words**. Sometimes words can be substituted for these nonverbal sounds in the framework of a game such as the ball game described above, so that the child says "boom" instead of "shhh" each time he throws the ball. Similarly, if Snap had previously been played with a tongue click each time both players lay down identical cards, now the players could say "snap."

Whenever possible, it can be very helpful to have **recordings of the child speaking** made with his family at home for use in the school therapy sessions, as this is a pre-direct speech way of having the child's voice present in sessions. If such recordings exist, they should be incorporated early on in the treatment sessions as a way of breaking the first barrier of hearing the child's voice.

At this transitional stage, the therapist can include recordings as a tool for relaying messages between herself and the child—the therapist may record questions and leave the room, and the child records the answers. Gradually, the child may go from speaking in a tape recorder, to speaking to the therapist when the therapist is standing outside the door, and then inside the room looking away, and, finally, looking towards the child.

Other ways of eliciting speech can be playing games that require whispering such as Chinese whispers, gradually shaping the whisper so that it becomes louder as the therapist moves further away from the child. If the child manages to whisper, the therapist could play games in which the whispering is amplified, such as having the child speak into a microphone.

Great patience is required to move gradually from one stage to the next. Care must be taken not to give in to the urge to rush ahead, as this might not only fail to bring the desired result, but it may also set the child back, as his feelings of competence could diminish and his anxiety level may rise.

Once the child is saying words in the sessions, the therapist should work toward more spontaneous and complex speech. This often occurs naturally in the course of conversation and activities within a warm, comfortable child-therapist relationship. Sometimes it has to be engendered through games and activities that require increasingly complex levels of speech. Such games can include I spy, twenty questions, Guess Who and Taboo. For additional suggested activities, see the Therapist's Manual.

Once the child is speaking to the therapist in a closed room in school, therapy can proceed to the generalization stages, as described in Stages 3 and 4 (pages 104-115) in the Therapist's Manual.

References for Further Reading

American Psychiatric Association. 2000. *Diagnostic and Statistical Manual of Mental Disorders*, 4th ed. Washington, DC.

Black, B., and T.W. Uhde. 1995. Psychiatric Characteristics of Children with Selective Mustim in a School-Based Sample." *Journal of the American Academy of Child and Adolescent Psychiatry* 34 (7): 847-856.

Chansky, Tamar E. 2004. *Freeing Your Child from Anxiety*. New York: Broadway Books.

Elizur, Y., and R. Perednik. 2003. "Prevalence and Description of Selective Mutism in Immigrant and Native Families: A Controlled Study." *Journal of the American Academy of Child and Adolescent Psychiatry* 42 (12): 1451-1459.

Johnson, M., and A. Wintgens. 2001. *The Selective Mutism Resource Manual*. Bicester, Oxford: Speechmark Publishing.

Kearney, Christopher A. 2010. *Helping Children with Selective Mutism and Their Parents*. New York: Oxford University Press.

Kristensen, H. 2000. "Selective Mutism and Comorbidity with Developmental Disorder/Delay, Anxiety Disorder, and Elimination Disorder." *Journal of the American Academy of Child and Adolescent Psychiatry* 39: 249-256.

McHolm, A. E., C. E. Cunningham, and M. K. Vanier. 2005. *Helping Your Child Overcome Selective Mutism or a Fear of Speaking: A Parent's Guide*. Oakland, California: New Harbinger Publications.

Rapee, R. M., H. J. Lyneham, C. A. Schniering, V. Wuthrich, M. J. Abbott, J. L. Hudson, and A. Wignall, (2006). *The Cool Kids® Child and Adolescent Anxiety Program Therapist Manual.* Sydney: Centre for Emotional Health, Macquarie University.

Rapee R., S. Spence, V. Cobham, and A. Wignall. 2000. *Helping Your Anxious Child.* Oakland, California: New Harbinger Publications.

Shipon-Blum, E. 2000. *The Ideal Classroom Setting for the Selectively Mute Child: A Guide for Parents, Teachers and Treating Professionals.* Philadelphia, Philadelphia, Pennsylvania: Smart-Center Inc.

Shipon-Blum, E. 2007. *Selective Mutism & Social Anxiety Disorder, Learning to Socialize & Communicate within the Real World. Audio CD.* Philadelphia, Pennsylvania: Smart-Center Inc.

Steinhausen, H., and C. Juzi. 1996. "Elective Mutism: An Analysis of 100 Cases." *Journal of the American Academy of Child and Adolescent Psychiatry* 35: 606-614.